P9-CSU-114

Unions
and
Free Trade:

Solidarity
vs.
Competition

by
Kim Moody & Mary McGinn

A LABOR NOTES BOOK
Detroit   1992

For Cleto Nigmo

A LABOR NOTES BOOK
Copyright 1992 by Labor Notes
First Printing: January 1992

Labor Notes is a monthly newsletter of labor news and analysis intended to help activists "put the movement back in the labor movement." It is published by the Labor Education and Research Project, which holds a biennial conference for all labor activists, acts as a resource center, and puts on schools and workshops on a variety of topics. See the inside back cover for more information on *Labor Notes* publications.

Permission is granted to unions, rank and file union groups and labor studies programs to reprint sections of this book for free distribution. Please send a copy of such reprinted material to Labor Notes, 7435 Michigan Ave., Detroit, MI 48210. Requests for permission to reprint for other purposes should be directed to Labor Notes.

Cover photo credits:
TOM LANEY, MATT WITT

Library of Congress Catalog Card Number: 92-070092
ISBN 0-914093-05-3

Contents

ACKNOWLEDGMENTS

This handbook is the result of many efforts to build networks of solidarity among workers in the U.S., Mexico, and Canada. It reflects the courage of everyday heroes to work towards a unionism without borders.

We have many people to thank who helped clarify the analysis and facts around free trade. Matt Witt of the American Labor Education Center wrote the section on allies in Mexico. Tim Costello and Elly Leary contributed the section on public employees in chapter 5. Others who helped: Ken Traynor, Common Frontiers; Duncan Cameron, Canadian Centre for Economic Alternatives; Laurell Ritchie, Confederation of Canadian Unions; Richard Balnis, Canadian Union of Public Employees; Adolfo Gilly, National Autonomous University of Mexico; Hector de la Cueva, CILAS; David Barkin, Autonomous Metropolitan University of Mexico; Jerry Tucker, UAW New Directions; Pete Kelly, UAW Local 160; Elaine Burns, *Guardian*; Mujer a Mujer; many staff and members of the Communications Workers of America; and friends from the Mexican Action Network on Free Trade and the Action Canada Network.

Many others shared their experiences of building links at the grass roots: Tom Laney, UAW Local 879; Baldemar Velázquez, Farm Labor Organizing Committee; La Mujer Obrera staff; Joe Fahey, Teamsters Local 912 and the Displaced Workers Committtee in Watsonville; Alex Dagg, ILGWU-Canada, to name only a few. We have had the privilege to work with these and many others on tours, conferences, and exchanges.

Simone Sagovac provided essential help with proofreading, corrections, and additions. David McCullough designed the book and did the layout. This is David's fifth book for Labor Notes.

We want to acknowledge the tireless work done by Jane Slaughter of the Labor Notes staff on improving this handbook as few other writer-editors could do. Jane is the author or editor of four other Labor Notes books. Her contributions to this handbook and her good humor throughout made the whole process a joyous act of collective labor.

We hope this handbook will enable unionists to learn from the examples of fellow U.S., Canadian, and Mexican workers, and will spur creativity and action to build true solidarity.

CHAPTER 1

Deregulating a Continent

Commerce between different regions of the world is as old as recorded history. The Assyrians and the Persians, the Chinese and the Indians, Romans and Greeks, Mayas and Incas, all traded with distant peoples. Today, no less than centuries ago, nations depend on trade. No country has the resources to be self-sufficient, so trade is not optional.

The North American Free Trade Agreement is not about the commerce of nations. This treaty that binds the United States, Canada, and Mexico in economic union is more about corporate profits than about trade. It is about letting private business reorganize the North American economy without the checks and balances once provided by unions, social movements, or governments. The North American Free Trade Agreement (NAFTA) would roll back a hundred years of controls and restrictions that were placed on private business in the interests of the majority of people.

WHY REGULATION?

Working people have fought long and hard to force governments to tame destructive business competition and limit the exploitation of labor. In the 1880s, the Knights of Labor and the American Federation of Labor fought for the eight-hour day. In the 1890s, populist farmers won government regulation of railroads. In the twentieth century the labor movement won for most workers the minimum wage, Social Security, and the right to collective bargaining. More recently, the civil rights, women's, and environmental movements won equal employment opportunities, affirmative action, and environmental standards.

Beginning in the 1970s, American business interests have worked to undo these many forms of regulation. They claim that regulations make them "uncompetitive." They say it is time to "get government off the backs" of business. They whine about government interference, although their rivals in Asia and Europe operate under far more government guidance. They have convinced (or bought) a generation of politicians and have already undone a great deal of the regulation that unions and social movements won during this century.

The North American Free Trade Agreement is the final accomplishment of a continent-wide deregulation which its framers hope will make U.S. corporations competitive with those of Japan and Europe. Their goal is to give the corporations total flexibility, all the way from the workplace floor to the world market.

In the workplace they seek to substitute team concept for union work rules and union power. In North America as a whole, they plan

FRUITS OF DEREGULATION

Deregulation is most advanced in the United States. Congress, the courts, or the President have lifted controls on airlines (1978), trucking (1980), railroads (1980), natural gas (1981 and 1985), banking (1980 and 1982), and telecommunications (1977, 1984).

Several major airlines are in bankruptcy court, with others operating in the red. Wages and working conditions have been battered throughout the industry. The 1989-91 Eastern Air Lines strike became the symbol of resistance to anti-labor employers exercising their freedom from government regulation. It was also a reminder of how disadvantaged labor is in a deregulated atmosphere.

In trucking, "the market" brought bankruptcies, buy-outs, new non-union giants like Overnite and J.B. Hunt, and the shrinking of once powerful national Teamster contracts.

In banking we saw the savings and loan bailout scandal (at a cost of about $5,000 per U.S. resident), a soaring rate of bank failures and mergers, and the near-collapse of some of the nation's largest financial institutions.

A 1984 consent decree broke the Bell System into several different companies. Here too, the unions experienced a new aggressive posture by AT&T and the "Baby Bell" operating companies.

---

to reorganize both manufacturing and service industries to make themselves "lean" predators in the global economic jungle. The NAFTA, in other words, is a policy in line with corporate interests in a competitive world.

For over a decade now, the governments of the United States, Canada, and Mexico have deregulated important industries in the belief that this would make their economies more efficient. They have lifted restrictions on pricing, on entry to certain industries, and on banking and financial practices; relaxed health and safety and environmental controls; and privatized government services. Freed of government interference, the theory goes, the market will set everything right and make the country competitive once again.

Deregulation often led to mergers and even bankruptcies. These helped many businesses to reorganize on a larger scale, often giving them greater power to resist union demands or unions altogether. The drive for concessions in the deregulated industries spilled over into others, reducing labor costs throughout much of the economy. If deregulation meant new problems for workers and consumers alike, for business it meant increased profits.

Simultaneously, employers stepped up their drive to recapture the workplace. Although the power of unions on the job has always been severely limited in the United States, the employers wanted total flexibility in workforce deployment. Work rules, seniority, grievances, and all the other aspects of "adversarial" unionism were targets in business' campaign to reorganize the workplace along lines pioneered in Japan. Attractively packaged as team concept or employee involvement, this reorganization sought to gut union contracts and put workers in competition with one another. These schemes would change the workers' loyalty to one another and to their union into loyalty to the company and its competitive goals.

The idea of free trade throughout North America was a logical extension of deregulation and "flexibility." Bringing Mexico and Canada into the deregulated atmosphere of the U.S. economy of the 1980s meant cheaper access to a wealth of raw materials, energy sources, and above all, Mexico's economically depressed workforce of nearly 30 million people. And all of this would be on terms established by U.S. business.

Another reason the idea of a North American free trade zone gained momentum in the 1980s was the formation of powerful economic blocs in Europe and Asia. Japanese companies began to move more of their production to lower-wage nations in East Asia, furthering regional economic integration. The twelve nations of the European Community agreed to end all trade and investment barriers by the end of 1992. This would create the Single European Market—until the NAFTA, the world's largest industrial power and market.

THE TREATY AND WHAT IT COVERS

George Bush's attempt to push through the NAFTA on the "fast track" was meant to leap over the Europeans by creating an even larger market. The fast track procedure meant that Congress would not be allowed to amend or even have extended debate over whatever treaty Bush brought back from negotiations. Congress could only vote yes or no. This meant that no regulations such as labor or environmental standards could be attached to the treaty. But what appeared to be a rush job was, in fact, the result of more than a decade of preparation.

The push for deregulation and the idea

NATIONS MUST CUT WAGES TO STAY COMPETITIVE IN THE WORLD MARKET...

...THE U.S. CUTS WAGES TO COMPETE WITH JAPAN, WHO CUTS WAGES TO COMPETE WITH KOREA, AND SO ON AND SO FORTH...

...UNTIL WORKERS EVERYWHERE EARN NEXT TO NOTHING AND CAN'T AFFORD TO BUY THE PRODUCTS PRODUCED...

...THIS IS KNOWN AS FREE TRADE!!

of North American free trade arose together in the United States in the late 1970s and grew throughout the 1980s. In 1979, Congress passed the Trade Agreements Act, calling on the President to study "the desirability of entering into trade agreements with countries in the northern portion of the western hemisphere."

In 1985, the idea of free trade between the U.S. and Canada was raised at the "Shamrock Summit" between Ronald Reagan and Canadian Prime Minister Brian Mulroney. By 1988, the U.S.-Canada Free Trade Agreement was signed. In 1987, the U.S. and Mexico signed a "framework understanding," and a more detailed agreement was signed on October 3, 1989. Negotiations on many details of the future treaty were already under way before most Mexicans or Americans had even heard of the idea.

California's World Trade Commission aptly summarized the U.S.

MEXICO IS ONLY THE BEGINNING

Corporate ambition will not stop at the Mexican border. Guatemala, for instance, already has 40,000 people working for a dollar a day in plants modeled after Mexico's maquiladoras. These plants serve U.S. firms such as Levi's and Guess, K-Mart and Sears. El Salvador and Nicaragua face economic restructuring that will eventually harmonize their ruined economies with that of North America.

In July 1990 George Bush announced the Enterprise for the Americas Initiative. This plan would eventually bring all of Latin America and the Caribbean into a free trade zone. Its conditions for membership are severe—countries must agree to an International Monetary Fund austerity and restructuring program. While the future of this initiative is uncertain, it warns us that U.S. corporations are willing to reach far and wide in their search for profits.

---

agenda for the NAFTA talks: "Both governments, in close consultation with the private sector and other interested groups, have defined the scope of issues to be put on the table. From the U.S. perspective, everything is negotiable except the free movement of labor." "Everything" includes matters usually thought of as domestic policies.

U.S. Trade Representative Carla Hills put forth these objectives:
1. Allow free flow of capital with minimal limitations on investment, including the right of U.S. corporations to return all profits earned in Mexico or Canada to the U.S.
2. Open previously protected Mexican services, resources, or industries (including oil exploration and refining) to U.S. investment.
3. Deregulate Mexican and Canadian banking, insurance, and transportation and open them to U.S. investment and ownership.
4. Make deregulation irreversible by specific inclusion in the treaty.
5. Privatize Mexican state-owned industries.
6. Assure compliance with U.S. standards of "intellectual property

rights" protection. The U.S. has the most stringent copyright and patent provisions in the world. This means that U.S. firms would continue their virtual monopoly over new technology, no matter where it is used.

7. Encourage greater integration of production in North America through "rules of origin" that guarantee a minimum proportion of North American content.

The goal is to bring Mexican and Canadian laws and economic policies in line with the U.S. vision of deregulation. The treaty is about opening Mexico and Canada to U.S. investment.

Ironically, points 6 and 7 actually *increase* regulation—showing that business has nothing against regulation when its interests lie that way. "Rules of origin" guarantee a high percentage of North American content in products traded within the bloc, but they disallow any laws guaranteeing that that content come from any one nation. This is to the advantage of the corporations that have the most money to invest—mostly U.S. corporations. It will encourage these firms to invest in Mexico.

To these specific points must be added the doctrine of "harmonization." This sweet-sounding concept, which will be embodied in the NAFTA as it was in the U.S.-Canada Free Trade Agreement, means that over time, the laws, taxes, social programs, and regulations of the three countries must be brought in line with one another. Since the NAFTA does not mandate higher standards, the tendency will be

for a downward harmonization.

Corporations will try to use the doctrine of harmonization to gut social programs (national health insurance, for example), labor laws, or environmental protections they consider to be "unfair trade practices." For example, through international settlement panels and through the court systems of each nation, corporations of one country can challenge any practice, program, or law that they say amounts to a subsidy of business in another country. (See chapter 4 for information on what has already happened in Canada.)

Finally, the NAFTA is to be a treaty. This means that all its provisions are unchangeable unless all nations agree to renegotiate. The purpose of making this economic pact a treaty is frankly stated in the U.S. International Trade Commission's report: "By codifying liberal trade and investment policies in an international agreement...a U.S.-Mexico FTA would increase the confidence of investors in Mexico's economy."

Consciously excluded from this treaty agenda are any references to labor rights, environmental protection, health or welfare standards, or labor migration. George Bush has told us not to worry, he will take care of these matters separately.

DIFFERENT AGENDAS

This highly unbalanced agenda makes it clear that the interests of the multinational corporations and of working people in all three countries are quite different. With no guarantees of labor rights, free trade between countries as economically unequal as the U.S. and Mexico is simply a license to exploit. Such a treaty with no environmental standards is a license to pollute.

The North American Free Trade Agreement is deregulation on an international level. It is a context in which corporations can run free in pursuit of profit without regard to the social, environmental, or overall economic consequences. For corporations it is a declaration of independence from the many regulations and policies that labor and other social movements have fought for over the years. It is ultimately less about trade than about corporate power.

We are at a turning point in the decades-old process of economic integration. It is a point at which the actions of organized labor matter. The impact of economic integration can be modified by a powerful, united, international labor response.

Because the implementation of free trade and international deregulation will occur over a period of years, we have some time to regroup and rebuild the forces of labor within our countries and across our borders. What we do not have is time to waste. The search for alternatives must begin now with a deeper understanding of what lies ahead and what we can do about it.

CHAPTER 2

Hitting Below the Sun Belt

In 1990 AT&T closed its New River plant in Radford, Virginia, putting 1,000 people out of work. The work done at New River went to Dallas, Texas and Matamoros, Mexico. Since that transfer, more and more of the Dallas plant's work has gone to Matamoros.

The New River workers and their union, the Communications Workers of America (CWA), were all the more shocked because they had made concessions in hopes of saving their jobs. CWA vice-president Jim Irvine told the *Washington Post*, "Radford really got to me because it was there that they took the cuts and some [wage] retrogression. The wages were among the lowest in the [AT&T] plants."

At $8.56 an hour, the New River workers were making well below the national average of $10.83 for manufacturing production workers. But William Warwick, president of AT&T's microelectronics division, coolly told the *Post*, "There was nothing the people in New River Valley could have done to offset the economic advantages of putting that work into Dallas [and Matamoros]. It was not a matter of their skills, their dedication or their efficiency. It was based on economics."

These "economics" are clear. Workers at the Matamoros AT&T plant make $1.15 a hour. Many others who work in Matamoros make $.50. The national average in Mexican manufacturing is $1.85 for wages and benefits. No amount of wage cutting, labor-management cooperation, or altered work rules by U.S. workers could match that. The CWA says it has lost 100,000 members at AT&T in the last decade, while the company has hired over 10,000 workers in low-wage countries.

AMY ZUCKERMAN/Impact Visuals

This maquiladora worker in Nogales makes 55¢ an hour. The plant provides cable systems and harnesses for AT&T.

Mexico is a special favorite of AT&T's because, as Warwick says, "The labor rates in Mexico are competitive with anybody in the world. It's lower cost than Singapore and competitive with Malaysia and Thailand." And, he might have added, it's a lot closer to the U.S. market.

AT&T's New River workers haven't been the only ones to lose their jobs to cold corporate calculations. A few examples:

- In 1988, 296 members of United Auto Workers Local 247 at TRW's Sterling Heights, Michigan auto parts plant took deep concessions to save their jobs. Local 247 recording secretary John Siino noted that "TRW stressed that we were a team." In 1991, TRW announced that the team's work would leave for Mexico.

- In 1988, workers at Schlage Lock's Rocky Mount, North Carolina plant learned their work would go to Mexico. These mostly African American women had no union and made about $8 an hour. With the help of a community-based organization called Black Workers For Justice, they fought the shutdown. In the end they won some severance pay and pension rights. But the plant was closed.

In 1991, some 400 workers in Watsonville, California, mostly women of Mexican origin, lost their jobs when Green Giant transferred their work to a non-union plant in Irapuato, Mexico. The Watsonville workers made $7.61 an hour plus benefits, while the women in Irapuato make about $.50 an hour with few benefits.

The same story could be told about tens of thousands of blue collar and white collar workers in the U.S. From the Rust Belt to the Sun Belt, low-wage workers, high tech workers, workers who make concessions, workers who cooperate with management, workers with and without unions are in danger of seeing their jobs move away.

INTERLOCKING ECONOMIES

Over the years U.S. corporations have invested more and more in Mexico and Canada. As a result the three economies have become increasingly interlocked.

U.S. DIRECT INVESTMENT

	1980	1988
In Canada	$45 billion	$61 billion
In Mexico	$7.7 billion	$14.9 billion

Sources: *Statistical Abstract of the United States*, 1990; David Barkin, *Distorted Development: Mexico in the World Economy*, 1990.

The rate of new U.S. investment in Mexico is growing every year—it was 10 times greater in 1989 than in 1982, rising from $266 million per year to $2.7 billion. The U.S. accounts for about two-thirds of all foreign investment in Mexico. U.S. investment in Canada is also growing.

By virtue of the size of its population and its wealth, the United States dominates this economic integration. The Gross National Product of the U.S. is ten times that of Canada and twenty-eight times that of Mexico, while its population is twice that of Canada and Mexico combined.

POPULATION AND GROSS NATIONAL PRODUCT

	GNP 1989	Population 1990
United States	$5,233 billion	250 million
Canada	$514 billion	27 million
Mexico	$192 billion	88 million

In terms of trade, both Canada and Mexico are already closely tied to the U.S., which is the largest trading partner of both countries.

U.S. DOMINATES NORTH AMERICAN TRADE (1988-89)

% of Canadian imports which come from U.S.	69%
% of Mexican imports which come from U.S.	64%
% of U.S. imports which come from Canada	20%
% of U.S. imports which come from Mexico	5%
% of Canadian exports which go to U.S.	78%
% of Mexican exports which go to U.S.	64%
% of U.S. exports which go to Canada	22%
% of U.S. exports which go to Mexico	6%

Sources: *Statistical Abstract of the United States*, 1990
The World Almanac, 1991.

THE RELOCATION DREAM VACATION

When AT&T's William Warwick talked about the "economics" of moving work to Mexico, he probably had more in mind than the obvious savings in production costs. Business, after all, isn't just about selling goods or services at competitive prices. Its reason for being is to make a return on investment—in other words, to make a profit. From this angle, competition means getting a better than average return. It is the economics of investment, as well as the economics of production, that matter to U.S. corporations.

By investing in Mexico a corporation gains in two ways: 1) The plant costs less to build because construction costs are 33-50% of those in the U.S. 2) The savings in wages allow the company to make back its investment much faster than it would in the U.S.

Take the example of Ford's stamping and assembly facility in Hermosillo, Mexico. Ford spent $500 million on this state-of-the-art complex, which opened in 1986. Total compensation for each of its 1,600 workers, including benefits and various social security taxes, came to $2 per hour. Thus Ford's annual wage bill was less than $7 million a year.

"I pledge allegiance to the flag of the country that gives me the best deal."

In contrast, total compensation for U.S. auto workers was about $30 an hour, so annual labor costs for the same size workforce in the U.S. would be almost $100 million. By building in Mexico instead of Michigan, Ford is making $93 million a year in extra profits. This extra profit alone will pay for the Hermosillo plant in a little more than five years.

No wonder a recent study by economists Alicia Giron and Edgar Amador of Mexico's National Autonomous University called Mexico an "investor's paradise." The rate of return on foreign investments in Mexico jumped from 55.9% in 1989 to 63% in 1990. Compare this with the rate of return in the U.S. in recent years: 7% to 12%.

Not surprisingly, foreign investment in Mexico is rising fast. In the first three months of 1991, foreign direct investment was $1.7 billion. In 1990, it had been $2.7 billion for the entire year.

It is this investment that creates much of the trade between the U.S. and its neighbors. It is this investment that the North American Free Trade Agreement (NAFTA) is designed to encourage.

A PARTICULAR KIND OF TRADE

The "trade" envisioned in the NAFTA is a very particular kind of trade—different from what we learned about world trade in our high school history books. In the textbook theory of international commerce, trade means "arms length" trade. A finished product is sold by an independent company in one country to a buyer in another country.

Most U.S. trade with Mexico, however, is trade *within the same company*, with a partly-owned subsidiary, or with a closely associated subcontractor. General Motors, for example, gets electrical components from a GM plant in Reynosa. Economists call this "intra-firm" (inside the firm) or "related-party" trade, and it is a relatively new type of trade. A more accurate name for it is "international out-sourcing."

A study in the *Oxford Bulletin of Economics and Statistics* estimated that about 71% of U.S.-Mexico trade is between related parties. In the last ten years the volume of this kind of trade has nearly doubled.

Until the 1980s, Mexico protected most of its domestic industries with high tariffs, import licenses, strict local content requirements, and quotas. Secure from foreign competition, Mexico developed a wide range of industries producing for its own internal market. For this reason, by the 1970s Mexico had become one of the more in-dustrialized Third World nations.

A major exception to Mexico's policy of protecting its domestic in-dustries was the "in-bond" or maquiladora agreement signed by the U.S. and Mexico in 1965. This program allows U.S. companies to import materials into Mexico duty-free for further processing or final assembly. These products are then exported back to the U.S., where the company pays only a small tariff on the value added in Mexico (labor, materials, and overhead). Since the labor is the main cost and is so inexpensive, the tariff is minimal. Most maquiladora plants are located on or near the border.

The maquiladora program was an early version of free trade. It was a bargain for U.S. manufacturers—so much so that employment in the maquilas grew from 119,000 workers in 620 plants in 1980, to more than 500,000 workers in 2,007 plants in 1990. Imports into the U.S. from maquila plants account for 45% of all imports from Mexico and were worth almost $12 billion in 1989.

The maquiladora program offered something else that attracted U.S. investment—wages far below the Mexican average. The vast majority of the first maquila workers were women, working in gar-ment or electronics plants. They were paid the minimum wage of about $.50 an hour, less than a third of the average wage in manufac-turing. Far from helping Mexican women, as some have claimed, maquila jobs reinforced their subordinate position in Mexican society.

Much of maquila production involves components that go into consumer durable goods like cars, computers, telephones, or household appliances. Of the four examples of job loss used above, two (AT&T and TRW) were component plants.

Maquila trade is called "trade" instead of "outsourcing" only because there happens to be a border between the various plants involved in assemb-ling the final product for market.

This outsourcing is a key part of the "lean" production system which is at the heart of the contemporary corporate strategy for competitiveness. It is described in the next chapter.

CHAPTER 3

Free Trade and Management-by-Stress

The "team concept" was the management mania of the 1980s. American manufacturers scurried to reorganize their production to become "lean and mean."

This chapter will explain how free trade and the team concept, or lean production system, work together. They are intertwined parts of management's agenda for the 1990s and the twenty-first century. Taken together, their effect is to weaken unions and downgrade working conditions.

The lean system was pioneered by Japanese companies, in particular Toyota. The country of origin is not terribly important—though it has fueled prejudice against the Japanese. What is important is that employers in other countries caught on fast. The lean system is now being put in place worldwide, in a host of industries: manufacturing, services, even education and government. The pressure is on for companies to adopt the lean system in order to become competitive. And they are trying to convince their workers to go along.

MANAGEMENT-BY-STRESS

Labor Notes has analyzed the lean system in *Choosing Sides: Unions and the Team Concept* (see chapter 12). We call this system "management-by-stress" (MBS), because the system itself—including the workers—are always stretched to their limits. It features:

- A "flexible" workforce: an end to union work rules, such as classifications and transfer rights. Management expects workers to perform many different jobs.

- Speedup.

- Deskilling of jobs so that workers are interchangeable.

- Constant pressure to find "smarter" (faster) ways of working (this is called *kaizen* in Japanese, or "continuous improvement"). Workers are expected to contribute suggestions for how they can do the job with fewer people.

- A two-tier workforce: more and more work is subcontracted to lower-wage firms.

- Linking of subcontracted work to the main plant by the just-in-time system of parts delivery and inventory. Suppliers deliver to the main facility just as their stocks are needed; no big inventories are maintained. Factories develop much more control over their suppliers than previously, forcing them to deliver on time, at a high quality

and low cost. This cuts costs on both storage and material-handling labor.

The management-by-stress system is hell on working conditions. Workers say, "My seniority doesn't mean anything anymore; there aren't any good jobs left." Jobs are overloaded. Toyota assembly workers in Japan, for example, perform 20 motions every 18 seconds or more than 20,000 motions a day. U.S. plants following the MBS model have high rates of carpal tunnel and other repetitive motion injuries.

The two-tier (or three-tier) workforce is key. As much work as possible is farmed out to lower-wage companies, almost always non-union. In addition to buying parts from outside, management wants to subcontract what it calls "non-value-added" work—any jobs not directly involved in production. This includes maintenance (both skilled and non-skilled), security, and material handling. The aim is to buy components, supplies, and services ready-made rather than building or performing them in-house. Just-in-time delivery of parts makes this multi-tiered system possible.

Some examples: An auto assembly plant buys its seat cushions pre-assembled from a non-union company. A state agency uses janitors from a $6-an-hour contractor. The Postal Service sends new automated work—bar code reading—to a private company. The workforce is pared down—lean—because much of the employer's work is now done elsewhere.

In the 1980s more and more manufacturers established subcontractors in Asia and Latin America. However, transportation costs, trade barriers such as tariffs and content laws, and other countries' limitations on foreign ownership ate away at the savings made on low wages. Free trade in North America was the answer. Canada's natural resources and Mexico's low wages, along with the geographic proximity of both, made them the natural partners in a free trade agreement directed at lean production.

The North American Free Trade Agreement will make international outsourcing and subcontracting even more economical and practical. The 1991 Economic Report of the President makes the goal of the NAFTA clear—outsourcing is at the heart of it:

> A free-trade agreement would boost the international competitiveness of both U.S. and Mexican firms. To reduce costs, companies often allocate phases of a manufacturing process among a number of nations. A free-trade agreement with Mexico would further encourage this natural international division of labor.

MBS IN MEXICO

Management is not satisfied with making huge profits from its Mexican plants simply by paying low wages. The plan is to run these plants under a management-by-stress regime as well. Ford's Hermosillo plant, for example, mentioned in chapter 2, was designed by Ford's partner, Mazda, and builds Tracers and Escorts under the "concepto de grupo" (team concept).

CONTINENTAL WHIPSAWING

In the U.S., the 1980s saw the spread of wage cuts and contract concessions of all kinds. National and pattern agreements that had standardized wages within many industries were eroded as one or another group of workers was forced to take concessions in hopes of saving their jobs. Standard wages and benefits were meant to prevent workers from having to compete with each other. They were a foundation of day-to-day solidarity. Concessions put workers into competition with one another—undermining solidarity and inviting further rounds of concessions. They further weakened a labor movement already in decline.

One of the strongest competitive levers corporations used to get concessions out of workers was whipsawing: playing one workplace against another. Management would threaten to move work if the workers in one plant didn't make their costs "competitive." All management needed was an alternative site of production—within the same company, at a subcontractor, or abroad.

The NAFTA makes it easy for companies to link Mexican plants into the system. It brings enormous wage differentials within common production systems and common employers. It will increase the corporations' ability to whipsaw.

HOURLY WAGE RATES IN US$, 1990

Ford production worker, U.S.	$16.50
Ford production worker, Hermosillo, Mexico	1.03
Ford production worker, Cuautitlán, Mexico	1.25
AT&T production worker, Radford, Va. (closed)	8.50
AT&T production worker, Matamoros, Mexico	1.15

HOURLY COMPENSATION RATES IN US$, 1990

Manufacturing production worker, U.S. average	$14.83
Manufacturing production worker, Mexico average	1.85
Manufacturing production worker, Mexican maquila	.50

To sum up our first three chapters:

- The North American Free Trade Agreement is primarily about U.S. investment in Mexico and, to a lesser extent, Canada. It accelerates the economic integration of the U.S., Canada, and Mexico already under way for decades.

- Free trade is part of the deregulation of the entire economy which business succeeded in winning in the 1980s. It will clear the way for U.S. businesses to go where they want, when they want, regardless of the social consequences.

- The growing "trade" with Mexico is really intra-firm outsourcing.

- The management-by-stress or lean production system depends on multi-tier wages; it is spreading across borders.

- The enormous wage differential between Mexico and the rest of North America expedites whipsawing. It creates the terrain for undermining living standards in all three nations by imposing a regime of constant competition among workers.

As bad as it sounds, workers and unions are not helpless in the face of these changes. In fact, economic integration creates some new opportunities for building and exercising union power. In chapter 8 we will talk about how unions can confront the effects of free trade.

CHAPTER 4

The Canadian Experience

In January 1989 the bilateral Canada-U.S. Free Trade Agreement went into effect, despite six years of public debate and organizing led by the Pro-Canada Network (now called the Action Canada Network—see chapter 7).

Three years into the Free Trade Agreement (FTA), Canadian working people were suffering one of the worst recessions since the 1930s. According to the Conference Board of Canada, it was also the first "made-in-Canada" recession, spurred partly by the FTA. The agreement resulted in reduced tariff intakes, increased taxes, and privatization of sectors of nationalized industries and services. Over 400,000 manufacturing jobs were lost in less than two years.

Until the Free Trade Agreement, Canada had certain regulations which gave it the right to manage its own natural resources; ensured that there was a "net benefit" to Canada from foreign firms operating there; ensured domestic production by firms wishing to sell in Canada; and guaranteed Canadian control of key sectors of the economy.

The FTA wiped out these rights.

U.S. corporations were granted the "right of establishment" and the "right of national treatment." This permitted them to build facilities, buy up existing businesses, or provide services in Canada on the same basis as Canadian companies. American companies have equal access to loans and resources.

On the other hand, Canadian companies did not gain unrestricted access to the U.S. market. The legislation passed by the U.S. Congress to implement the FTA actually gave U.S. companies new ways to take

Downtown Toronto

DAVE HARTMAN/Impact Visuals

action against Canadian exporters suspected of using "unfair sub-sidies."

In addition, it appears that there was a secret side deal to the FTA, to increase the value of the Canadian dollar. U.S. corporations had long charged that the weaker Canadian dollar was an unfair subsidy which allowed Canadian business a competitive advantage. After the agreement was signed, the Canadian dollar rose from US$.72 to US$.86—a result of high interest rates set by the Bank of Canada. Canada's trade balance with the U.S. switched from a $4.8 billion surplus in 1986 to a $5.8 billion deficit in 1990.

The FTA set the stage for dramatic changes in the welfare of the Canadian people, everything from cuts in the national health care program to reduced investment to decreased unemployment bene-fits. In this chapter, we will look at the effects on jobs, social services,

---

NO LOVE FOR FREE TRADE

Free trade has never been popular in Canada. Even in 1988, when the Conservatives ran—and won—promising that free trade would bring "jobs, jobs, jobs," 57% of the voters voted for the two anti-free trade parties, the Liberals and the New Democratic Party. (Canada's three-party system means that a party can win a majority of seats in Parliament with a less than majority vote.)

The Conservatives then took advantage of an obscure power, never used before, to stack the Senate with eight new appointed Senators, giving them a majority in both houses of Parliament and ensuring that they could pass whatever legislation they wanted.

---

natural resources, the environment, and culture. Much of what has occurred in Canada, a country of equal per capita wealth but one-tenth the population of the U.S., is a keyhole view into the future: what will happen to working people in the U.S. as the corporate agenda roars further south in search of lower wages and standards.

JOB LOSS

From June 1989 to March 1991, Canada lost 435,000 manufactur-ing jobs, or 21.7%. Although some percentage of this loss can be attributed to Canada's overall recession, it was free trade that helped to initiate that recession. The economic dislocation is "at least as wrenching as the U.S. Rust Belt experienced in the early 1980s," says Andrew Jackson, senior economist of the Canadian Labor Con-gress. "It's been a real shakeout here."

The corporate restructuring unleashed by the FTA includes both U.S. takeovers of Canadian plants and the relocation of Canadian plants to the U.S., mergers, plant closures, subcontracting, and bankruptcies. Before, Canadian companies had far less incentive to move their plants to the U.S. Sun Belt. Now companies are lured by low wages and lower costs of property, taxes, real estate, and transportation, and there are no tariff barriers to hold them in Canada. Buffalo alone, across the border from Ontario, has attracted 86 Canadian companies since July 1987. But much work has also moved further south to the unorganized regions of the U.S. and to maquiladoras in Mexico.

The business owners who move their plants are the lucky ones. Many are declaring bankruptcy as smaller and medium-size Canadian companies find themselves uncompetitive with U.S. transnationals. *Canadian Dimension* reports that 9,407 companies went under in the first ten months of 1991, up 25% from the same period in 1990, and up 41% from 1988, before the FTA. And plant closures mean permanent job loss.

Percentage of Laid-off Canadian Workers Whose Layoffs Were due to Plant Closures:

1982	21.5%
1989	55.4% (first year of the FTA)
1990	48.2% (second year of the FTA)

Source: Andrew Jackson, "Job Losses in Canadian Manufacturing: 1989-91," figures from the Ontario Ministry of Labour.

Many Canadian firms have been bought out by U.S. companies. In 1988-89, 460 were taken over by foreign owners (primarily Americans). During the same period only 136 foreign-controlled businesses—worth only a tenth as much—were taken over by Canadians. More than 90% of foreign corporate activity in Canada is in the form of takeovers, not new investment.

WHO BENEFITS?

With the harm to Canada so obvious, why is the Conservative Party government pushing the free trade agenda to its limits? As in the U.S., free trade does benefit someone—the largest corporations. The irony is that in Canada, these are largely subsidiaries of American firms.

The bilateral Free Trade Agreement came about because U.S. corporations wanted to get rid of Canadian policies that protected energy resources and controlled foreign investment in Canada. Canadian executives, like executives everywhere, were thoroughly in tune with the desire to undermine any regulation of business and to increase its mobility. The Business Council on National Issues, made up of CEOs of large companies and patterned after the Business Roundtable in the U.S., argued for free trade as a way to make Canada—that is, their firms—"competitive."

Among other things, the executives wanted to get rid of Canadian social programs they saw as too expensive. But in order to justify such alterations in the Canadian way of life, they had to bring in outside pressure—free trade—to enforce competitiveness.

Manufacturing jobs in auto parts, textiles, clothing, food processing, and electrical and electronic assembly have been hit the hardest.
Women are concentrated in these industries (except auto), in particular women of color, immigrants, older women, disabled women,
and women with low levels of education.

Auto is Canada's most important industry, providing many spin-
off jobs as well as those in parts and assembly plants. Under the

---

MAKE CONSUMERS PAY

As tariffs have been dropped at the border, the Canadian government has lost $2 billion a year. This shortage was passed on to
consumers in the early stages of the FTA when the Conservatives
pushed through a 7% federal sales tax, the Goods and Services Tax
(GST)—while polls registered opposition from 80% of Canadians. The
Action Canada Network calls the GST the "free trade tax."

U.S.-Canadian Auto Pact, auto companies had to maintain at least
60% Canadian content in Canadian-made cars, and, essentially, to
build one car in Canada for each car sold there. The companies com-
plied with these rules to avoid paying the penalty, a tariff on
imports. The FTA phased out the tariffs, limiting the rule to only
50% *North American* content to ship cars from the U.S. to Canada.
Under the NAFTA, North America of course includes Mexico. There
will be no enforcement for strictly Canadian content.

In the last two years companies have announced the elimination
of 16,000 auto jobs. Forty-three parts plants, many represented by
the Canadian Auto Workers, have closed.

Service jobs may be the next to go (84% of service workers in
Canada are women). The FTA was path-breaking for business in that
it was the first trade agreement in the world to bring service industries under the discipline of such a treaty. Free trade in health
and professional services was included under the FTA, and in the
NAFTA negotiations, banking and telecommunications were on the
agenda.

SOCIAL SERVICES

Canada is known for providing social services for its people, from
national health care to comprehensive unemployment coverage. In
the drive for a level playing field (lowest common denominator), the
government is drastically reducing these services.

Only a few months after the FTA was signed, federal contributions to unemployment insurance were eliminated. Benefits were
cut, eligibility was tightened, and fewer weeks of benefits were
granted. Canadian unionists say it is remarkable how closely the new
Canadian regulations resemble the stingier U.S. system.

Although Prime Minister Brian Mulroney promised that adjustment programs, including retraining, would be available to those whose plants closed because of free trade, in fact $100 million was shifted from the unemployment insurance commission into private sector training.

Medicare, Canada's national health care program, is also on the chopping block. Previously, the federal government set standards which the health program in each province had to meet in order to receive federal matching funds; two cornerstones were little or no cost to the user and portability from province to province. Then Parliament decided that all federal money towards Medicare would be phased out over five years. This meant not only a big cut in health care funding, but that provincial governments were free to enact user fees or deny claims from other provinces.

In addition, a few hospitals in Canada are now run by American private firms.

The future promises more competition from the private sector. For example, U.S. daycare chains can claim "unfair competition" from the provincial governments' non-profit daycare centers. Free trade will even allow U.S. private education firms to compete for access to public funds for training programs in Canada. The Canadian Teachers Federation expects that "publicly-supported elementary and secondary school systems across Canada will face increasing pressure to conform more closely to their generally less adequately funded and less equitable U.S. counterparts."

NATURAL RESOURCES AND THE ENVIRONMENT

One clause in the FTA gives the U.S. equal access to all of Canada's energy resources—oil, gas, electricity—even if Canada has a shortage, and at the same price that Canadians pay. Access to water is also included.

Besides eliminating national sovereignty over resources, the FTA has meant the lowering of environmental standards. The treaty says that neither party may adopt standards that create unnecessary obstacles to trade.

- In British Columbia, with its large forestry industry, public funds were used to support replanting trees. The province abandoned the program after it was challenged by the U.S. as an "unfair subsidy." The U.S. argued that both the regulation requiring replanting and the fact that the province subsidized the program made it difficult for U.S. forestry companies to compete.

- In a last-ditch attempt to have some say over the export of natural gas, the National Energy Board of Canada rejected U.S. companies' export licenses. When the companies appealed to the Canadian Federal Court, the NEB abandoned its position in fear of financial retaliation. The U.S. company line, as described by Steven Shrybman in *Earth Island Journal*, was that "Canada had no authority under the FTA to prevent energy exports simply because the costs to Canada were greater than the benefits."

Extensive energy projects are already under way to serve the U.S. market. The controversial James Bay II hydroelectric project will flood vast areas of northern Quebec. It will mean the destruction of the Crees' and Inuits' way of life and wreck the ecology of the region.

Shrybman points out that limitless access to cheap energy is not, in the long run, a boon to the U.S. either. The U.S. currently consumes 25% of the world's energy, with just 6% of the population. Largest consumers of that energy include transnational corporations. "These energy mega-projects," says Shrybman, "...flooding the States with cheap natural gas and electricity from Canada, will only prolong the inefficient use of non-renewable resources."

CULTURE

Many Canadians have long resented the American domination of their culture, from television to movies to products of all types. "Our ability to control the dialogue between Canadians depends on national television and radio," explains Ken Traynor of Common Frontiers in Toronto. "Free trade in cultural items means we just can't compete. There have been cuts of over $100 million to the CBC—TV and radio—which means regional and local programming gets chopped.

"The U.S. negotiators define culture under services. We fight back as a sovereignty issue—they treat it as a commodity like anything else."

Any preference to Canadian authors, actors, or national media can be challenged by the U.S. as an unfair subsidy. Canadian author Rick Salutin reports, "A bill introduced in the American Congress said that if the Canadian government passed this very mild bill to protect Canadian film distributors in Canada, the United States would penalize Canada not only the amount of dollars it lost in Canada, but the amount of money it lost anywhere in the world where countries introduced similar legislation—on the grounds that Canada had set a bad example and was responsible!" Canada withdrew its original proposal.

The U.S.-Canada Free Trade Agreement has had devastating effects in Canada, and it shows in the polls. In late 1991 the Conservative Party government had only a 12% approval rating.

The government has implemented the policies described here despite tremendous opposition. Both the devastation and the opposition are certain to grow when, under NAFTA, the "level playing field" includes Mexico.

CHAPTER 5

Free Trade Hits the United States

In this chapter we will present the worst-case scenario: what will happen in the U.S. if the corporations are successful in carrying through their plans under the NAFTA. Their plan is nothing less than to reorganize North American industry. We can expect:

1. The "hollowing" of industrial production. This means that the bulk of a company's work is done by subcontractors.
2. Loss of manufacturing jobs.
3. Job loss in service industries as telecommunications, financial services, and transportation follow manufacturing.
4. Corporate reorganization through mergers, divestments, bankruptcies, and joint ventures.
5. Intensified pressure for contract concessions and management-by-stress.
6. A weakened economic base in a number of regions and communities.

THE GEOGRAPHIC IMPACT

The regions most likely to lose jobs because of the NAFTA are the U.S.-Canadian Rust Belt (Quebec and Ontario down through the Midwest); the "industrializing" belt of the South that runs from Tennessee through North Carolina; high tech centers like Boston and Silicon Valley in California; areas of labor-intensive manufacturing like Los Angeles and many of the industrial border towns; and communities based around food processing, pulp and paper production, furniture making, and cement production.

The impact on service jobs will be more geographically dispersed, but it will likely slow down the growth in service jobs that took place in the 1980s.

MANUFACTURING MIGRATION

The largest job losses due to the NAFTA are certain to be in manufacturing. A recent study by economists from the University of Massachusetts and Skidmore College predicts that between 260,000 and 439,000 U.S. manufacturing jobs will be lost between 1992 and 2000. A study by the labor-supported Economic Policy Institute projects the loss of 500,000 jobs in the same period.

Which industries will feel the impact of free trade first? The NAFTA is to be phased in over time. The complete elimination of trade and investment barriers for different products may take from one year to fifteen. But assuming some similarities with what happened under the U.S.-Canada pact, the first to be hit will be the more labor-intensive industries, particularly garment subcontracting. Since these manufacturers do not need to invest in expensive machinery—only sewing machines in the case of garment work—they can relocate rapidly. A 1989 joint communique points toward garment work as a priority for the NAFTA negotiations (along with textile, auto, and steel).

The table below shows the industries most likely to lose jobs; they account for a third of the manufacturing workforce.

U.S. INDUSTRIES LIKELY TO LOSE JOBS DUE TO FTA IN 1990s

MANUFACTURING	Employment	% Women	% Black	% Latino
Autos and Parts	1,191,000	19.8%	14.6%	4.7%
Household Appliances	168,000	40.0%	11.3%	1.7%
Garment	993,000	77.8%	15.5%	23.7%
Consumer Electronics	32,000			
Computers and Software	289,000	40.8%	7.9%	7.0%
Electronic Components	561,000	(4 electrical categories combined)		
Telecommunications Equipt.	110,000			
Cement	19,000	8.3%	13.5%	10.7%
Food Processing	1,701,000	32.6%	12.9%	12.1%
Furniture	685,000	20.9%	11.1%	8.5%
Pulp and Paper	323,000	16.6%	9.1%	3.2%
Textiles	714,000	47.1%	24.8%	4.9%
Steel	370,000	7.8%	13.1%	5.4%
Oil Refining	158,000	19.9%	12.6%	3.4%
SERVICES				
Telecommunications	1,274,000	41.5%	13.1%	5.4%
Banking	2,008,000	71.1%	9.7%	6.4%
Insurance	2,314,000	61.2%	8.1%	4.6%
Trucking	1,831,000	13.6%	11.6%	5.5%
Total	15,429,000			

Sources: *Handbook of Labor Statistics*, Bureau of Labor Statistics, 1989
U.S. Industrial Outlook, Dept. of Commerce, 1991.

Next to move will be relatively light manufacturing, but more capital-intensive and/or high tech: food processing, consumer electronics. Not far behind will be telecommunications equipment, other electronic equipment, and textile products.

In the case of the steel industry, companies will not build new plants in Mexico. But one study indicates a 10% loss of U.S. production to existing Mexican mills in the next several years.

A more long-range process is the major reorganization of auto and truck assembly described in chapter 9. The Big Three auto makers are pushing to abolish trade barriers immediately, and parts production is certain to accelerate its migration. Larger investments will take a little longer, but the Big Three and the Japanese already have plans to build new assembly plants in Mexico.

Although it may take longer than the relocation of labor-intensive industries, ultimately the migration of capital-intensive

IMPACT ON UNION TOWNS

The unionized sections of the country will be particularly hard hit by the NAFTA.

About 23% of manufacturing workers, or 4.5 million, are represented by unions. Of the 15 states with above-average percentages of union members in manufacturing, 11 are in regions vulnerable to free trade. These 11 more highly unionized states (Illinois, Indiana, Maryland, Michigan, Missouri, New Jersey, New York, Ohio, Pennsylvania, West Virginia, and Wisconsin) account for nearly two-thirds of all union membership in U.S. manufacturing.

These 11 states were already badly bruised during the 1980s. Five hundred thousand union members in manufacturing lost their jobs from 1984 through 1989; nearly two-thirds were from these states.

industries will have the biggest impact on jobs in the U.S., because they will draw suppliers and services around them in Mexico.

This will be possible because U.S.-owned final assembly plants in Mexico will no longer be required to buy their parts in the U.S., as they were under the maquiladora program. The desire for just-in-time delivery *within* Mexico will push this process.

SERVICE DRIFT

As manufacturing migrates to Mexico, services that are closely linked to it will follow. Factories require banks for financing and payrolls, data transmission for electronically linked production and inventory systems, increased phone or electronic mail contact with the home office, more direct air transport for executives and sales personnel, and dependable truck and rail transport for their products. Many of these services can be done at less cost, closer to the production site, in Mexico.

In addition, even services for companies located in the U.S. can be transferred electronically. Data processing and storage is an obvious example. Long done in the Caribbean for U.S.-based firms, corporate data can be compiled, processed, and stored off-shore, and then transmitted electronically as needed to the home office. This sort of work is increasing in Mexico.

Even before the signing of the NAFTA we find Southwestern Bell investing in Mexico's major phone company, TELMEX. U.S. banks are deeply involved in Mexico as holders of public and private debt and financers of businesses. Now they want to develop Mexico's new credit card business. Even U.S. trucking firms have opened operations in Mexico, including Roadway and J.B. Hunt. The NAFTA will further open these service industries to U.S. investment.

PUBLIC SERVICES AND PUBLIC EMPLOYEES

Free trade will hurt both public services and public employees by further eroding the business tax base, already diminished because of

FROM LOW PAY TO NO PAY

IMPACT ON WOMEN WORKERS

Women workers are a large proportion of the workforce in several of the industries likely to be hit hard and soon by the NAFTA: garment (77.8%), textiles (47.1%), electronic-related products (40.8%), household appliances (40%), and food processing (32.6%). Garment and textiles alone account for over one million women's jobs in the U.S.

Most of these are labor-intensive industries in which production has already begun migrating to Mexico.

Other women workers will be affected by the slowdown in the creation of new service jobs. For the last decade or more, service industries have accounted for most of the growth in employment in the U.S. and have made it possible for millions of women to enter the workforce. The drift of services to Mexico will diminish the opportunities for women entering the labor market in the 1990s.

IMPACT ON AFRICAN AMERICAN WORKERS

Free trade will be particularly hard on African American workers for two reasons: the regions and the industries affected. At least half of the 31 million African Americans in the U.S. live in the Rust Belt or in the newer Southern industrial belt, both of which will lose many jobs.

Just over 10% of the employed workforce is Black. As the table on page 23 shows, many of the industries likely to be hit by free trade employ above-average proportions of Blacks. Garment, textiles, food processing, and auto alone account for almost three-quarters of a million African American jobs.

The increased outsourcing under management-by-stress has already removed much production from urban areas with large Black populations. We can expect the subcontractors to continue to locate in predominantly white, rural areas in the upper South and lower Midwest.

IMPACT ON LATINO WORKERS IN THE U.S.

Among the first to be hurt by free trade will be the Mexican and Chicana women working in garment and electronics plants along the U.S. side of the border. There, relocation can take only a few days or weeks with relatively little investment. As Cecilia Rodriguez, former director of La Mujer Obrera in El Paso, Texas, put it, "The companies are lined up at the border waiting for the free trade gun to go off."

All of the following are both early candidates for job loss and major employers of Latino immigrants: large garment centers in Los Angeles, Chicago, and New York; electronics plants along the border, in California, Massachusetts, and elsewhere; food processing in the West. Farm laborers will be displaced as imports of Mexican fruits and vegetables increase.

Latino workers are also well represented in other industries likely to lose jobs: furniture, cement, electrical equipment, steel, and auto.

corporate flight from traditional industrial areas. In 1957, corporations accounted for about 45% of local tax revenue, but in 1989, they provided barely 15%. The corporate tax base has also been cut by competition between states and cities trying to attract or hold business. Trade delegations from states and cities scour Europe and Asia seeking new industry, promising tax abatements and infrastructure improvements.

For example, efforts to get Toyota to locate a plant in Kentucky saddled the state with a debt of $280 million over the next 20 years. In addition, most of Kentucky's federal job training money went to training Toyota workers. In the end each job cost $50,000. We can expect more of this desperate "smokestack chasing" under NAFTA.

Even as the local business tax base shrinks, federal aid to states and cities, adjusted for inflation, has been cut in half. At the same time, state and local payments for desperately needed health, welfare, and other safety net programs have continued to swell. Many of these programs are federally mandated but state and local governments are forced to foot the bill. This cost shifting has led to an increasingly regressive tax structure which has helped ignite tax revolts by workers and homeowners.

The deregulation rhetoric of free trade says that business taxes must be lowered if the U.S. is to be competitive. Public services, wholly dependent on those taxes, and the public employees who provide them will be the victims of this cost-cutting.

WHAT ABOUT U.S. EXPORTS TO MEXICO?

Despite its 88 million people, exports to Mexico are not expected to grow all that much. Hence few jobs will be created in the U.S. or Canada to serve the Mexican market. A recent study at the University of Texas estimates that U.S. exports to Mexico will increase by $3.6 billion in the next ten years when adjusted for inflation. But that is far less than the growth that occurred in the 1980s—about $6.5 billion.

One reason is the poverty and youth of Mexico's population. Nearly 40% of the population is under 15 years old. The per capita income is about $2,000 a year, one-tenth that of the U.S., half that of Korea. Only 10% of the adult population can afford U.S.-produced consumer goods.

The regions of the U.S. most likely to benefit from free trade are Texas and southern California. Half the projected exports will be from Texas, which already accounts for about 40% of all U.S. exports to Mexico. But the university study says that these exports will be from capital-intensive industries in Dallas, Houston, and Austin. Thus even in Texas, job creation will be small and limited to three cities. It will be offset by the jobs lost from the garment and light manufacturing plants in cities like El Paso and San Antonio.

The only aspect of the NAFTA that might create some new jobs in the U.S. are the "rules of origin." These state that a certain percentage of products or a proportion of the content of a product must originate in one of the three countries of North America. This could force some Asian or European companies that now export goods to the U.S. to build plants here. On balance, however, the U.S. is certain to experience a net loss of jobs.

MORE MERGERS AND BIGGER BUSINESS

The struggle for global competitiveness that drives free trade will bring about waves of international mergers, buy-outs, divestments, bankruptcies, and joint ventures. These will increase the size of the most successful corporations and further remove them from their original national identity and government control.

This process isn't new. *Business Week* calls it the rise of the "stateless corporation." U.S. corporations are already producing more and more of their goods abroad. These numbers tell the tale: In 1965, 17.1% of all the exports in the world were manufactured in the United States. By 1985, the U.S. share of exports had fallen to 13.4%. But the share of exports made by U.S.-owned corporations (operating around the world) actually rose during that time, from 17.3% to 18.3%.

Ever larger, stateless corporations operating in a deregulated international market present serious problems for workers and unions in all three countries of North America. They reduce employment by eliminating or combining operations; break up established contract patterns; reduce the proportion of workers represented by any one union; and use their global resources to break local strikes or organizing drives.

Since these business consolidations will be international in character, they will combine a large number of units with very different labor costs. This will increase the potential for internal and international whipsawing. The pressure on U.S. conditions will be enormous.

While the centralization of business power generally creates a more unfavorable balance of forces for workers, it also has a positive side. Centralization brings workers throughout North America under one roof. Just as the formation of giant national corporations a century ago first set local labor movements back, it also laid the basis for the growth of industrial unionism and national contracts.

What is laid out here is a worst-case scenario. If the labor movements in the three countries get their respective and joint acts together soon enough, they can affect the way business reorganizes. As we will discuss in chapter 8, the lean production system has its own points of vulnerability, and competition is a two-edged sword.

CHAPTER 6

Mexico: Winner Or Loser?

In the debate over the North American Free Trade Agreement, all sides seem to agree that Mexico will be a winner in the continental economy of the future. George Bush says everybody wins. Mexican President Carlos Salinas de Gortari sees the NAFTA as Mexico's invitation into the First World of fully developed industrial economies. Opponents of free trade, such as the AFL-CIO, see lost American jobs as Mexico's gain. The assumption is that no matter what happens elsewhere, Mexico will profit as a nation.

This is wrong. As we will show, the jobs created in Mexico will be a drop in the bucket compared to the jobs lost there because of free trade. And the new jobs pay less than those destroyed. Because many will be organized according to management-by-stress, they will be harder as well.

In the early 1980s the Mexican government decided on a drastic restructuring of the economy, designed to open Mexico to U.S. corporations. This restructuring has made Mexico an investors' paradise, but it has meant more poverty for the Mexican people.

MEXICO'S TRANSFORMATION, PHASE I

In the 1960s and 1970s, Mexico became one of the first wave of Third World "economic miracles." The miracle consisted of high average growth rates—6% or more a year from 1965 through 1980. The industrial sector grew even faster at 7.6% a year, expanding from 27% of Gross Domestic Product in 1965 to 35% by 1985. The adult illiteracy rate fell from over 25% in 1970 to about 10% in 1985, well below that of most Third World nations.

Like Brazil and South Korea, Mexico produced not only raw materials, agricultural products, textiles, and other typically Third World products. It also made automobiles, electrical appliances, computers, and other modern consumer goods. Although U.S. companies played a big role in this modernization, most of this new production was for Mexican consumption, not for export.

The Mexican government played a big role in the country's industrial development. The state owned nearly 1,200 enterprises, including the airlines, the telecommunications system, and the oil recovery and refining industry. The government also assisted the agricultural sector and the food distribution system.

Mexican workers benefited during this period of industrialization. Workers' real monthly earnings doubled from 1960 to 1978. From 1975 to 1981, average hourly wages and benefits of production workers in manufacturing grew from $2.00 to $3.71. This was largely the result of labor militancy. (Some of these gains were later wiped out by inflation in the early 1980s.)

Mexico's miracle, however, was not without problems. For one thing, the ruling Institutional Revolutionary Party (PRI in Spanish) used many of the government enterprises for patronage; its politicians often skimmed personal wealth off the national treasury. For another, by the early 1980s much of Mexico's plant and equipment was behind world standards—unsuited for the era of competition it was about to enter. But most serious of all was Mexico's debt problem.

To industrialize, Mexico had to import most of its capital goods—factory machinery, computer systems, and other equipment—from the U.S. It paid for them with loans from big banks, also mostly in the U.S. These banks were more than happy to pour money into Mexico, with its valuable oil exports and high profits. But during the 1970s interest rates soared, making these loans more expensive. Oil prices eventually crashed, depriving Mexico of important income with which to pay off the loans. These problems were compounded as Mexico's elite sent some of the borrowed capital abroad "for safekeeping." By 1982 Mexico was up to its border in debt.

The miracle had turned into what Mexicans call "la crisis."

TRANSFORMATION PHASE II

Everyone knows that most Third World countries are badly in debt. So are most of the richer First World countries, including the U.S. and Canada. But the institutions which are managing the debt crisis—the World Bank and the International Monetary Fund—are controlled by the rich countries. So they not only demand repayment from the poorer countries, but impose drastic austerity programs to make sure that payments are made.

Mexico was never allowed to design its own way out of its debt crisis. From the 1980s through the present, the Mexican government's economic programs have been devised to meet the demands of the International Monetary Fund (IMF) and the U.S. banks.

The government agreed to try to pay off the debt by lowering the living standards of the Mexican people. It adopted an acute austerity program that froze wages, cut social spending, reduced food subsidies and farm credit, privatized state enterprises, and regeared both agricultural and industrial production from domestic consumption to exports.

Mexican officials saw the turn toward manufactured exports as the way to pay off the debt. But it was also a way for the IMF, U.S. corporations, and the Mexican elite to drag Mexico into the international economy—as the perfect location for American and Canadian runaway shops.

Responding to pressure from Washington, in 1986 Mexico agreed to open its economy to foreign investment and the world market by joining the General Agreement on Tariffs and Trade (GATT). In 1987 Mexico and the U.S. signed the framework agreement that was the forerunner of the NAFTA. One result was the tripling of manufactured exports by the end of the 1980s—most of them to the U.S. But there were other results as well.

One was a steep drop in Mexican living standards. Whereas per capita Gross National Product had risen about 4% a year from 1965 to 1980, it fell by almost 3% a year during the 1980s. The real national minimum wage, which had risen steadily from the early 1950s into the late 1970s, was cut in half during the 1980s. The average wages and benefits of manufacturing workers fell from their historic high of $3.71 per hour in 1981 to $1.85 by 1990. Auto workers who made $5 an hour in 1981 were lucky to get $1.25 by the end of the decade. The newer plants and maquiladoras paid much less.

George Bush and Carlos Salinas looked on their work and smiled. The Fortune 500 smiled. It was time for the NAFTA.

JOBS, CITIES, AND THE ENVIRONMENT

The austerity-plus-exports plan of the 1980s delivered on two points: it increased manufacturing exports by over 300% and it created some 400,000 new maquila jobs, along with several thousand more in other export-oriented projects like Ford's Hermosillo and Chihuahua plants and the steel complex at Cuidad Lazaro Cardenas. A generous estimate of new manufacturing jobs for this period might be about half a million. This, however, was only one side of industrial restructuring.

The other was the mass destruction of jobs in the older industrial sectors. In just five years (1982-87), 700,000 jobs were wiped out. Some 200,000 of these were the result of privatization; many state enterprises were either merged or liquidated. Many private sector jobs were lost because imports replaced locally produced consumer goods, older production systems were modernized, and declining incomes undermined the domestic market. Total job loss for the decade probably ran close to one million.

In other words, more jobs were lost than created in this period of restructuring.

One consequence was the growth of Mexico's already large "informal sector." The visible tip of this underground economy was the growing number of women street vendors to be seen in the squares and plazas of Mexico's cities. Perhaps a quarter of women working outside the home are in the informal sector, where there is no minimum wage and no health care.

The half a million who got the new jobs were the lucky ones, but only by comparison to the unemployed. They faced living conditions few would envy. The swelling maquila cities along the border are evidence that investment and development are not the same thing.

From Matamoros in the east to Tijuana in the west, these are cities without an urban infrastructure. For the plants and new office buildings there is water, energy, pavement, even well-kept green areas. The corporations pay no taxes to support either the services they receive or to provide city services for the rest of the community. As a result, in the neighborhoods where the workers live there are no paved streets, proper sewage systems, or running water.

Even worse is the environmental damage. The government has adopted what environmentalists call the "rich then clean" approach. That is, first you industrialize an area, and later, when the money is flowing in, you clean up the mess. The U.S. government has the same approach, but is rich enough to start cleaning up toxic wastes (when pressured). Mexico is not. So, despite laws as stringent as those in the U.S. (including the requirement to abide by U.S. standards within 100 miles of the border), Mexico's environmental crisis has spread with new investment.

Mexico's best known environmental catastrophe is its capital, Mexico City. The air is toxic. Twenty million people live there, largely because of the earlier concentration of industry in the Central Valley of Mexico. The government's solution is to decentralize industry by encouraging investment outside the Central Valley, particularly along the border.

This has not solved the problem, however; it has simply extended the pollution to new regions.

WHAT LIES AHEAD FOR MEXICO?

What lies ahead is more of the same. Increased U.S. investment will bring the "maquiladorization" of Mexico. More U.S.-owned low-wage plants exporting to the U.S. and Canada, effectively making Mexico a supplier economy. More urban growth without proper services. More pollution.

In fact, Mexico's economic restructuring by unbridled market forces has only begun. There are literally millions more "uncompetitive" jobs to be destroyed. These include the small farmers on the traditional communal lands belonging to native peoples and on cooperative farms (*ejidos*). They account for half of Mexico's cultivatable land.

The end of government low-interest credit for the ejidos, the diversion of subsidies to large agribusiness farms, and the turn of agriculture toward world markets will mean the ejection of countless peasant families from the land. Their undercapitalized farms simply cannot compete with the giant agribusiness mega-farms that produce for export and attract both Mexican and foreign private capital. A leader of the conservative National Action Party (PAN in Spanish) estimates that as many as 15 million people could be

ITT produces cables for Ford and Chrysler near Matamoros.

thrown off the land and into the labor market by the end of the century. To this must be added the one million young people who already enter the labor market each year.

It is clear that the creation of half a million or even a million maquila-type jobs over the next eight or nine years will be only a drop in this sea of unemployment and poverty. The NAFTA and the integration of Mexico into world agricultural markets will bring with them a social catastrophe for which no North American government has any solution or fall-back plan.

Very few people in Mexico believe that closer economic integration with the U.S. can be stopped. But there are many who believe it can and must be controlled and that Mexico's development must remain under Mexican control—not the control of some "settlement panel" that can declare communal land ownership an unfair trade practice.

The next chapter describes our allies in Mexico and in Canada.

CHAPTER 7

Allies In Canada And Mexico

Workers in Mexico, Canada, and the United States all stand to lose from the North American Free Trade Agreement. Even what it seems to give with one hand—some jobs in Mexico—it takes away with the other, creating nightmare poverty and working conditions. It lays the basis for endless whipsawing.

The positive side to the NAFTA is that it makes it easy to identify our common enemies: the multinational corporations and the politicians who serve them. It is clear that in the new continental economy, workers in all three countries have common needs: secure jobs, higher incomes, health and safety protection on the job, and environmental protection in our communities.

For the long-term fight to win these things, we need a strategy of solidarity. This chapter will deal with allies in Canada and Mexico and describe what they are already doing to deal with free trade.

MATT WITT

Ford Cuautitlán workers.

Short-term coalitions for immediate goals can often be based on mutual interest alone, but durable alliances call for more. This is even truer when the allies are from different countries and cultures, speak different languages, have different labor traditions, and must deal with different political systems.

Even in seemingly similar cultures like those of the U.S. and Canada, people often use the same words to mean different things. When the differences involve language, as among those in North America who speak English, Spanish, and French, matters can be even more difficult. Add in everyone's sense of national pride and the differences in economic well-being, and the number of toes to be stepped on multiplies.

Solidarity, therefore, must be based on mutual respect for each other's nationality, culture, traditions, and language—as well as race, ethnicity, and gender. This is not a matter of abstract "political correctness," but of practical alliance building. It must be clear that we are building an alliance of equals.

Each of the union movements in the three respective countries brings different strengths to this fight. American workers bring their central position in the multinational corporations that dominate the new North American economy. But we also have much to benefit from and learn from unionists in Canada and Mexico.

Mexican workers bring not only a recent history of labor militancy, but a tradition of revolutionary nationalism that makes radical solutions appear far more realistic than they would in the U.S.

The Canadians have a strong trade union movement relative to their national economy. Over 36% of all workers are unionized. More than American unions, they have resisted concessions and the mentality that goes with them. They have a labor party, the New Democratic Party, and are more involved in alliances with other social movements than American unions are.

ALLIES IN CANADA

In Canada, the anti-free trade forces are organized into a strong coalition whose member organizations represent more than ten million Canadians. They have been working together for six years, since before the bilateral U.S.-Canada Free Trade Agreement (FTA) was signed. The Action Canada Network (formerly the Pro-Canada Network) is made up of over 50 national organizations, including unions, environmental groups, women's organizations, religious groups, and social justice organizations.

The ACN tried to stop the FTA through mass media educational campaigns to convince the public to put pressure on the government. The Network took out full-page newspaper ads and distributed a comic book describing the effects of the FTA. In the 1988 elections, a majority voted for the two parties which opposed the Free Trade Agreement. But Brian Mulroney's Conservatives won a plurality in Parliament and kept control of the government.

After the FTA went into effect in January 1989, the Network produced a piece of literature titled "Told You So!" which contrasted the government's predictions with the actual results of free trade.

Now the ACN is campaigning to abrogate (cancel) the bilateral FTA and to keep Canada from signing the trinational NAFTA. One of its slogans is "Free Canada, Trade Mulroney." The bilateral treaty includes the right for either government to cancel the deal with six months' notice. However, the NAFTA, if signed, will supersede the U.S.-Canada FTA and thus eliminate this option.

The organizations within the Network emphasize different ways of combatting the effects of free trade, but they all agree on one thing: abrogation of the treaty. Their work includes: building trinational links with counterpart organizations in the U.S. and Mexico; pressure on the Mexican government to carry out democratic elections and respect human rights; development of a "social

CANADIAN LABOR MOVEMENT STATS:

- Percentage of workforce in unions: 36.5%
- Labor confederations:
  Canadian Labour Congress (CLC). 2.3 million workers, 58.6% of all unionists
  Confederation des syndicats nationaux (CSN). 5.3%, primarily in Quebec
  Canadian Federation of Labour (CFL). 5.2%, mostly construction unions
  Confederation of Canadian Unions (CCU). .8%
  Associations. 21.7%, primarily teachers and nurses
- Largest unions:
  Canadian Union of Public Employees (CUPE) 376,900
  National Union of Provincial Government Employees 301,200
  United Food and Commercial Workers 170,000
  Canadian Auto Workers 167,400
- Union members who are women: 37.2%
- Decentralized collective bargaining: 24,725 separate agreements in 1987 (bargaining units of 100 or more)

charter"; and election of the anti-free trade New Democratic Party.

Here we will mention some of the representative organizations in the Network and their demands.

Unions. Some unions have made contacts with their counterparts in Mexico and the U.S.:

- The Canadian Auto Workers were very active in supporting the Ford Cuautitlán workers in Mexico, and the CAW national office has committed to consistent information exchange with GM, Chrysler, and Ford locals in the U.S. and Mexico (see chapter 8). A General Motors local passed a resolution to set up a GM Solidarity Network in Canada for trinational contacts within GM.
- The International Ladies Garment Workers Union of Canada has made ties with the September 19th Garment Workers Union in Mexico.
- The British Columbia Federation of Labour sponsored a speaking tour of Mexican trade unionists.
- The Communication Workers of Canada has formed an alliance with unions in the U.S. and Mexico (see chapter 10).

New Democratic Party. The Action Canada Network is nonpartisan, so the NDP is not a member. But many see the election of the NDP, which is strongly supported by labor and controls three provincial governments and the Yukon Territory, as the key to abrogating the U.S.-Canada deal. NDP victories in Ontario in 1990 and British Columbia and Saskatchewan in 1991 indicate that a growing segment of the population is fed up with the Conservative government, including its strong pro-free trade stand. The next national election is in 1993.

DAVE HARTMAN/Impact Visuals

A union float in the Toronto Labour Day parade.

Women. The National Action Committee on the Status of Women (NAC) is the largest feminist organization in Canada, with over 530 member groups nationwide. NAC has published "What Every Women Should Know About Free Trade" and established a subcommittee to make sure women's issues are included in the work against free trade. Besides sponsoring forums and conferences in Canada, it helped organize a trinational women's conference in Mexico in February 1992.

Human rights groups. These organizations demand that the Canadian government pressure the Mexican government to allow democratic elections and respect democratic rights. The Latin American Working Group, for example, called for the government to send monitors to Mexico to observe the 1988 presidential election in an effort to help prevent fraud.

Cancel the debt. ACN member groups say that Mexico's foreign debt should be annulled. The British Columbia Working Group on Canada-Mexico Free Trade, for example, calls on Canadian banks to "set an example of international economic development and generosity by forgiving the $4.9 billion debt owed by Mexico....The people of Canada can afford to do this."

Social Charters. Some groups have designed social charters, or declarations of human rights, as an alternative to the NAFTA. They are thinking through how integration of the three economies could be put at the service of people rather than corporations. The Ecumenical Coalition for Economic Justice, an alliance of churches, has published such a charter. The approach to agriculture, for example, would "begin with a recognition of peoples' right to basic food self-reliance."

Allies in Canada are easy to find. With six years of organizing against free trade, they have a wealth of experience in analysis, research, and local efforts; now they are promoting trinational

exchanges and alliances. And they are clear about their purpose:
This debate is not about Canadian workers opposed to Mexican workers, this is about multinational corporations not caring about workers. We oppose the idea of Mexican workers being played off against Canadian workers while corporations reap the profits.

—CLC President Shirley Carr, May 1991

ALLIES IN MEXICO

As in Canada, there exists in Mexico a national network of anti-free trade organizations, the Mexican Action Network on Free Trade (RMALC in Spanish). It includes unions and environmental, women's, and religious groups. The Action Network hosted a tri-national conference in 1991 which is described in chapter 8.

The Mexican labor movement is divided on the question of free trade. Union leaders who are allied to the country's ruling party support the NAFTA. Independent and democratic union movements generally do not.

Most unions are tied to the Institutional Revolutionary Party (PRI), which has ruled Mexico for more than 60 years. In the 1930s, PRI established the Confederation of Mexican Workers (CTM) as its official arm in the private sector, and the Federation of Public Workers Unions (FSTSE) as its arm in the public sector. (Several smaller private sector federations are also allied to the PRI, including CROM, CROC, and COR.)

As a condition of employment, workers in many industries and public agencies have dues automatically taken from their paychecks, both for their PRI-linked union and for the party itself. Workers covered by the official federations are often bused to demonstrations supporting PRI policies and to the polls on election day to vote for the party's candidates.

In return for their political support, leaders of such unions are allowed to profit personally from collecting dues income—often from workers who do not even know they belong to a union. PRI-allied union leaders may also receive government contracts for businesses they own, as well as positions in local, state, or national government.

Workers in the maquiladora industry in the eastern part of the border region, around Matamoros and Reynosa, belong to the CTM, but in other maquiladora zones several federations are present and most workers are non-union. In the auto industry, workers are divided into a series of unions, some part of the official federations, others covering only one plant. Farm workers belong to many different federations, some more closely tied to the PRI than others.

A few major unions, such as the Mexican Telephone Workers Union (STRM) and Mexican Electrical Workers Union (SME), are not affiliated to official federations, but their top officers are closely allied to the PRI government. These leaders, along with the head of the National Union of Education Workers (SNTE), describe themselves as "independent," "modern," and "democratic," but do not stray from the PRI party line and do not support the independent and democratic movements.

Unions independent of PRI control are difficult to form because they must receive government approval in order to be legally registered. Nonetheless, a few truly independent unions do exist.

The oldest and largest independent grouping is the Authentic Labor Front (FAT), which involves about 40,000 workers in clothing, textile, auto parts, metalworking, universities, and other sectors. Although hampered by repression and lack of funds, FAT has a number of organizing drives going in maquiladora plants.

One well-known independent union is the September 19 Garment Workers Union, formed after the 1985 earthquake in Mexico City and made up almost entirely of women. The union's fight for legal registration benefited from international support and outrage over government fraud and negligence in the wake of the earthquake.

Because of legal obstacles to forming new unions, many workers have organized movements for democratic control of the official unions. CNTE, the democratic movement within the national teachers union, is the largest of these. In 1989, CNTE organized a nationwide wildcat strike of a half million teachers demanding decent pay and union democracy. As a result, CNTE supporters won control of the locals covering the states of Oaxaca and Chiapas and Mexico City's elementary and preschool teachers.

Movements in recent years by telephone workers, workers at the Ford Cuautitlán plant, Modelo/Corona brewery, Aeromexico, and the Tornel rubber company are other examples of efforts to win membership control of official unions.

• Positions On NAFTA

Leaders of the PRI-allied unions support their government's position on the NAFTA. Fidel Velázquez, head of the CTM, for example, has publicly criticized U.S. and Canadian unions for opposing it. In international meetings, the CTM has argued that raising wages above current levels would be bad for Mexican workers because transnational corporations could no longer afford to keep the maquiladoras open.

The heads of the telephone, electrical, and teachers unions also defend the NAFTA, while asking for a greater role for themselves in the negotiations. They have all lobbied their union counterparts in the U.S. with the idea that the NAFTA should include a "social charter." While this idea is supported by some Canadian and American unionists, it is opposed by others who fear that it would legitimate a treaty they don't want in the first place, and that it would go unenforced.

Independent and democratic labor movements, meanwhile, are

nearly unanimous in opposing the NAFTA. They are among the most active participants in the Action Network, in particular the FAT, the university workers (STUNAM), a small union of telephone technicians, the federal fishery department's union, some groups active in democratic movements in the teachers' and telephone workers' unions, and the labor committees of two political parties, the Party of the Democratic Revolution (PRD) and the Revolutionary Workers Party (PRT).

- ## Goals Of The Network

The Network's primary focus has been educational work and outreach to organizations not yet involved. The only information that most Mexicans receive about the NAFTA comes from government statements and industry advertising campaigns on television, which is controlled by PRI supporters. Salinas's message is that the NAFTA will "bring Mexico into the First World," allowing the Mexican people to enjoy the same standard of living as people in the U.S. Opposition statements do not appear on television at all. Thus, few Mexican workers have been exposed to the view that the NAFTA will mean more poverty and not new prosperity.

Democratic union movements have made opposition to the NAFTA a focus of small demonstrations on May Day and other traditional days of protest. Given the repression they face and their lack of access to the mass media, it is unlikely that they will be able to mount large-scale mobilizations in the foreseeable future. They are concentrating instead on

building the independent and democratic labor movement, which is key to change for Mexican workers over the long term, and on encouraging opposition political parties—particularly the PRD and PRT—in their work against the transnationals' agenda.

In addition, independent and democratic movements are building relationships with U.S. and Canadian unions. Representatives have participated in conferences on the NAFTA in the U.S. and have hosted binational or trinational conferences in Mexico. They have taken part in tours or meetings, for example:

- The September 19th Union has sent members on speaking tours in the U.S. and hosted an international women workers' conference in Mexico City.

- Activists in CNTE, the democratic teachers' movement, hosted a tour of U.S. teachers; conducted a speaking tour to California, visiting unions and schools and appearing on a number of radio programs; took part in a meeting of the National Coalition of Education Activists; and visited schools in Milwaukee. One result has been the establishment of "sister school" relationships.

- Workers from the Mexican telecommunications industry toured U.S. and Canadian cities to discuss with their counterparts the impact of free trade and technological change. They helped organize a trinational union conference in Mexico (see chapter 10).

- Representatives of FAT have taken part in U.S. conferences on health and safety and environmental protection.

- The Border Committee of Women Workers (CFO) has helped host several visits by members of the Amalgamated Clothing and Textile Workers, the United Auto Workers, and other unions to see conditions in the maquiladora plants and surrounding communities. (See chapter 8 for other examples of solidarity work.)

In building ties with U.S. and Canadian counterparts, Mexican unionists have tried to:

- Show working people and politicians in those countries that there is Mexican opposition to the NAFTA.

- Acquaint potential allies with conditions in Mexico.

- Encourage their counterparts to put more emphasis on the effect of the NAFTA on immigrant workers in the U.S.

- Ask U.S. and Canadian allies to pressure the Salinas government—which is very conscious of its international image—to enforce labor rights and accept political democracy.

- Emphasize common interests rather than competition among workers in the three countries.

More people enter the United States from Mexico than from any other country. Mexicans come to the U.S. because unemployment is three to four times higher there and wages are a tenth or less.

American unions have usually opposed the free flow of workers into the U.S. But this policy is harmful to workers in both countries, as the box on the next page explains.

HOW RESTRICTING IMMIGRATION HURTS ALL WORKERS

First, it enables American employers to super-exploit Mexican immigrants in the U.S., thus pulling U.S. wages and conditions down.

The argument usually given for opposing free immigration is that immigrants would depress wage levels as they competed with U.S. citizens. In practice, however, immigrant labor usually flows into the lowest paid jobs. Since most of these jobs are protected by the minimum wage, immigrants cannot "bid down" wages *if the minimum wage laws and other labor laws are enforced.*

However, as we know, these laws which apply to all workers, documented and undocumented, often are not enforced in workplaces with large numbers of immigrants. Employers get away with appalling violations of safety standards, overtime laws, and minimum wage laws because immigrants are wary of calling on enforcement agencies. To call attention to themselves, they fear, could mean deportation.

The Immigration Reform and Control Act of 1986, also known as the Simpson-Mazzoli bill, requires employers to demand documentation from job applicants to show that they are legally allowed to work in the U.S. It includes fines for employers who break this law. Thus someone with a job has a strong incentive not to get fired, since, without papers, it will be difficult to find a new one. Their lack of mobility makes immigrants unwilling to blow the whistle on lawbreaking employers.

If all workers were "legal," this downward pull on the conditions of minimum wage jobs would be much weaker.

It is not true, however, that immigrants don't mind working under degrading conditions. The Justice for Janitors victory in Los Angeles in 1990 and other campaigns have shown that immigrant workers will form unions when they believe they will be able to hold on to their jobs.

LOW-WAGE HAVEN

The second reason that keeping Mexican workers out hurts American workers is that it helps to maintain Mexico as a low-wage haven for U.S. business. With the Mexican labor market sealed off from higher U.S. wages (even if the seal is an imperfect one), there is no upward pull on Mexican wages.

In the maquila plants along the border, workers earn a fraction of the wages paid in U.S. plants only minutes away. No one would work for $.50 an hour if they could easily and legally make $4.25 only a few hundred yards away. If there were no restrictions on migration to the U.S., employers operating in Mexico would have no choice but to raise wages enough to hold on to their workforces.

If George Bush were consistent in his free trade ideology, he would have to support free immigration as part of the NAFTA. But he is consistent only in supporting what will benefit U.S. corporations. Maintaining restrictions on immigration helps to keep Mexico a giant "right-to-work" zone where labor is caged, but business is free to roam at will.

CHAPTER 8
Solidarity Strategies

I see silver threads, stretching across the country
starting in Mexico and going everywhere.
The thread is thin like the web of a spider
but strong like tensile steel.
Other threads are added and, given time, a cloth is formed
stretching from cities in Mexico to Canada.
The sound moves among the threads—stronger now.
The sound is solidarity.
—*Karyl Dunson, Oil, Chemical and Atomic Workers*
October 1990, Taxco, Mexico

We know what's coming down the fast track, we know who is
responsible, and we know who to count on as allies in Mexico and
Canada. But where do we start? Fortunately, there is already a good
deal of activity going on, including work by human rights, environmental, and women's groups. This chapter will discuss what union
activists can do.

Unions have taken several different approaches to free trade.
Some have concentrated on trying to defeat the NAFTA in Congress.
Others have worked to amend it with a code of conduct for corporations operating in Mexico, including labor rights and environmental
standards. Others have sought to impose a code of conduct, or social
charter, through direct pressure on the corporations or through use
of the provisions for labor rights which already exist in U.S. trade
laws. All of these approaches are worth doing.

We all know, however, that corporations routinely break labor,
health and safety, and environmental laws, and get away with it. So,
while a code of conduct for corporations is desirable, we still need a
trinational labor movement capable of enforcing it.

This leads us to a strategy of direct international organization and
action—a solidarity strategy. Our focus is on building trinational
union networks capable of confronting corporate power.

This chapter will present four case studies of workers and unions
that have begun to build cross-border solidarity. Then it will outline
some steps local unions can take, beginning with the easy ones and
looking toward the future. It will discuss the new weaknesses of the
corporations in the decontrolled economy of North America, and
end with some thoughts on political action.

LONG-TERM GOALS OF THE SOLIDARITY STRATEGY

1. The most basic goal is the eventual convergence of wages, benefits,
   working conditions, and living conditions for workers in all three
   countries—*upward harmonization*. It is based on the tendency of
   workers' wages to rise in developing nations when the economy as a

COMPETITIVENESS KILLS

The first step toward a North American solidarity strategy is to reject the whole philosophy of "competitiveness." Competitiveness is the buzzword of the 1990s, and far too many union members, seeking to survive, have taken this corporate outlook for their own.

"The need for competitiveness" is nothing new: businesses have competed in markets for hundreds of years. But competitiveness is one of those loaded words that implies a specific program of action. In this case, the program is for the union to adopt company goals.

The competitiveness philosophy prides itself on championing the new—new ways to produce, new ways to work, and new ways to think. It is a philosophy filled with positive words like pro-active, cooperation, smartness, flexibility. After all, who wants to be reactionary, contrary, dumb, and rigid? But the positive list of brand-new do's conceals a long list of very old don't's.

Don't question company goals. Don't rest on the job. Don't put your health before that of the company. Don't seek more leisure time. Don't expect your income to rise like it used to. Don't feel solidarity with your fellow workers—unless they are on the same team striving for company goals.

At the core of the competitiveness philosophy is the idea that workers should engage in dog-eat-dog competition in the workplace, just as corporations do in the world market. But competition kills. It kills businesses—60,000 or more go out of business every year in the U.S. alone. It kills jobs, communities, and the environment. In the workplace it is people who die or are maimed—in the U.S. about 11,000 occupational deaths a year and nearly two million disabling injuries. The competitive 1980s brought us new industrial diseases such as repetitive motion injuries that scarcely existed before. In Japan, where management-by-stress competitiveness is most developed, a phenomenon called *karoshi* (instant death from overwork) has appeared.

The heart of union philosophy has always been the opposite idea. An injury to one is an injury to all. We stick up for one another because it's right and because it's the best way to offset the power of management.

But human solidarity is not only morally superior to the law of the jungle; it is a matter of practical necessity for working people. Solidarity is how we raise our incomes and improve our working conditions over time. Solidarity is how we defend our health, our very lives on the job. Solidarity, not competition, must be the basis of any union strategy in the integrated economy of North America.

whole expands, *if* labor is able to organize. This was the case in Mexico prior to the 1980s. It is the case today in South Korea and Taiwan where, from 1982 to 1990, hourly wages and benefits rose 381.2% and 228.3%, respectively, under the pressure of new militant unions.

2. Upward harmonization requires a continuous raising of human and labor rights, social welfare, and environmental standards in all of the countries covered by the free trade agreement. While historically Mexico has had the most extreme difficulties, conditions are eroding in the United States and Canada as well. In each country we need to win or preserve:

- a shorter work week
- national health care
- rising minimum wages.

3. Cancelling Mexico's debt to U.S. banks would help working people in all three countries, because the debt is the reason for Mexico's austerity plan and strategy to increase exports. The debt is therefore a barrier to upward harmonization.

4. Upward harmonization must also occur *within* each of the countries of the NAFTA. The persistence of low-wage or non-union areas—such as the U.S. South—is a drag on the process of raising living standards overall. American unions need to mount an aggressive organizing drive to raise living standards throughout the country.

5. Economic integration must be approached in a new way—as an opportunity for development. See the box on page 53.

CASE STUDIES IN SOLIDARITY

Until very recently, on-going international labor solidarity was rare. But in the last few years more and more unions and rank and file workers have reached across borders. Their beginning steps are usually small ones, compared to the gigantic task of taming multinational corporations. But they are inspiring and point to the steps we will need to take before the 1990s get much older.

We present here four case studies, and follow them up with some suggestions for steps unions can take.

- **A Local Union Solidarity Committee: UAW Local 879's MEXUSCAN Solidarity Task Force**

Workers at Ford's St. Paul, Minnesota truck plant had their first encounter with the Mexican labor movement when Marco Antonio Jimenez visited St. Paul in April 1990. Jimenez was a member of the elected negotiating committee at the Ford Cuautitlán plant just outside Mexico City. He, like the rest of the committee, had been fired for resisting wage cuts and trying to change the leadership of their union. He told the St. Paul workers how, three months earlier, armed thugs had beaten and shot at workers inside the plant, with Ford's complicity. Dozens were injured and one, Cleto Nigmo, was killed. Jimenez was touring the U.S. to build support for their fight.

Jimenez made an impression on the members of United Auto Workers Local 879. In October, Tom Laney, the local's recording secretary, and José Quintana, a worker in the trim department, attended a trinational conference in Mexico. The conference set Laney and Quintana ablaze.

When they returned to St. Paul, they wrote the first in a series of articles for the Local 879 newspaper, talking about conditions in Mexico. They wrote, "After 10 years of immersion in Ford's programs which have turned U.S. workers against U.S. workers, we should agree that it's time to try the Union solution of international solidarity as a reasonable alternative for job security."

The executive board endorsed the formation of a MEXUSCAN Solidarity Task Force composed of board members and all interested rank and filers. It helped organize the trinational Ford Workers Justice Day on January 8, 1991. On this day workers in some Ford plants in Canada, the U.S., and Mexico wore black ribbons commemorating Cleto Nigmo's death.

Soon, 879 officials began doing some unusual things. Shop Chair Ted LaValley got up at a quality award ceremony, in front of Ford's North American chairman, and talked about Ford's collusion in the shootings. Vice-president Rod Haworth testified before the International Trade Commission about the treatment of Mexican Ford workers. LaValley introduced Cuautitlán worker José Santos to UAW Subcouncil 2, made up of reps from all U.S. Ford assembly plants. The local sent Tom Laney to the Ford stockholders meeting, where he confronted Chairman Harold Poling on the company's complicity in the armed attack.

The Task Force helped organize a two-day educational conference on the NAFTA, open to union and community activists. The turnout for this first effort was actually disappointing to the organizers—they had expected 200 people. But it established Local 879 as a leader on the issue of free trade in Minnesota. The Task Force went on to help organize the Minnesota Fair Trade Coalition.

It wasn't always easy going, according to Tom Laney. Some members thought the local ought to "stick to things inside the plant." But the shop floor reps pointed out that it was impossible to take care of things at home when Ford could whipsaw with ease. With persistence, trinational solidarity work found a legitimate place in

A SHORTER WORK WEEK

Since 1985, unionized workers throughout Western Europe have reduced the work week to 35-37 hours in most industries—at 40 hours' pay. In the U.S. and Canada the basic 40-hour week hasn't changed in half a century. In Mexico, the work week in manufacturing is typically 48 hours.

To save jobs in all of North America, we need a contractual or statutory work week of 35 hours with no loss in pay. This would raise Mexican hourly wages by about one-fourth. It would also spread work and soften the impact of industrial reorganization and relocation.

LABOR COMPETITIVENESS SCOREBOARD
. . .OR THE "SUCKER CURVE"

You say your paycheck buys less and your benefits don't cover what they used to? You say you work faster and put in more hours?

Well, cheer up, you're getting competitive.

That's right. Your slumping wages and your increased output per hour are the key to making your employer competitive. And you, the American factory worker, have done it.

Now, this does not mean that you are competitive with workers in Third World countries, where your employer threatens to outsource production. But Third World employers are not the real competition. By getting competitive, you have helped General Motors, General Electric, General Mills, and the rest of the U.S. corporate brass take on their European or Japanese counterparts in the world market.

Exports, the stuff of which the world market is made, come mostly from businesses based in rich countries. Seventy-five percent of their value comes from the 24 wealthiest nations who belong to the Organization for Economic Cooperation and Development (OECD). The U.S., Germany, and Japan alone account for a third of the world's exports.

U.S. corporations may buy parts from Asia and Latin America, but it is the giants of Japan and Europe with whom they compete.

WHO DOES THE EXPORTING?

1989	Merchandise Exports In $	World Market Share
World	$2,902.3 billion	100%
OECD 24	$2,173.6 billion	75%
(U.S.)	($346.9 billion)	(12%)
4 Asian Tigers	$202.1 billion	7%
Latin Am. & Caribbean	$112.0 billion	4%
Rest of world	$414.6 billion	14%

Source: World Development Report, 1991, World Bank.

In this competition, U.S. factory workers have done their bosses proud. After being the highest paid workers in the world for decades, U.S. factory workers have moved down the ladder. In hourly wages and benefits they are only about 15% ahead of Japan and Britain and below most European countries

Hourly Wages and Benefits in Manufacturing, 1990

Germany	Sweden	Italy	France	U.S.	Japan	Britain
21.30	20.93	16.29	15.25	14.83	12.84	12.42

Source: Bureau of Labor Statistics, 1991.

WORKING HARDER FOR LESS

From 1982 to 1990, real hourly wages and benefits (adjusted for inflation) fell 3.5% in the United States, while rising 18.4% in Japan and 26.9% in Germany. At the same time, U.S. manufacturing workers' productivity rose as much or more than most: 36.6%, compared to 38.1% in Japan and 24.8% in Germany.

As a result, the U.S. was the only major economic power to see a drop in unit labor costs during the 1980s. Unit labor costs fell 3.5% in the U.S. from 1982 to 1990, while rising 67.4% in Japan and 75.8% in Germany.

THE SUCKER CURVE

The Bureau of Labor Statistics has assembled all this data into a chart that deserves to be called the "sucker curve."
The straight line represents the unit labor costs of 12 nations

Chart 1. U.S. manufacturing unit labor costs relative to 12 competitors, 1973-90

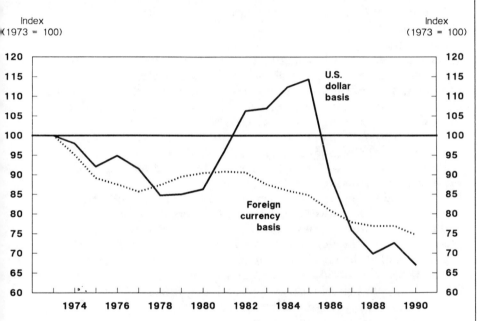

designated "competitors" by the BLS. The dotted line represents U.S. unit labor costs compared to those costs in the 12 competitors, measured in terms of their own currencies (yen, marks, francs, etc.). Measured this way, U.S. workers have been getting cheaper since 1974.

Even when measured in dollars, U.S. labor costs have fallen well below those of other nations, except during the mid-1980s when the value of the dollar was unusually high.

Chances are your employer did not show you the sucker curve when he asked for your cooperation, work rules, medical co-payments, or wage cuts. Feel free to show it to corporate executives, joint program facilitators, cooperative union officials, and other competitiveness philosophers.

the union's affairs.

Local 879 members can be found at conferences and actions promoting international solidarity all across North America. Two representatives attended the first trinational auto workers conference, held in Mexico (see below).

In November 1991, Local 879 got a strong indication that its solidarity work was irritating the powers-that-be. The fired Cuautitlán leaders were negotiating with Ford over severance pay, with the involvement of the Mexican government. President Salinas's office demanded that the workers drop all contact with Local 879. The workers refused.

- **International Corporate Campaign:**
  IBT Local 912's Giant Slayers

  Free trade began in food processing long before the NAFTA, as Mexico moved toward exporting cash crops and the U.S. relaxed old restrictions on agricultural imports. By 1990 Mexico was producing 60% of the frozen vegetables sold in the U.S. Watsonville, California, once known as the frozen food capital of the world, had lost over 2,000 jobs since the early 1980s.

  A majority of the members of Teamsters Local 912 in Watsonville are Mexican or Chicano, and its cannery and frozen food members are mostly women. In May 1990, Green Giant laid off 382 cannery workers in Watsonville; the work would go to its plant in Irapuato, Mexico. The Watsonville workers made $7.61 an hour plus benefits; in Irapuato the rate was $.50, with few benefits.

  The laid-off women, organized as Trabajadores Desplazados (Displaced Workers), launched a national boycott of Green Giant products, called the Campaign for Jobs, Justice, and Environment. Green Giant is a subsidiary of British-owned Grand Metropolitan— the 13th largest British corporation on *Business Week's* Global 1,000 list. Grand Met also owns Burger King, Haagen Dazs and Pillsbury, and the boycott was extended to them as well.

  The Displaced Workers Committee visited the plant in Irapuato and talked with the workers—also women. The Mexican workers had no union, so it was difficult to establish an on-going alliance. But the campaign produced a video, *Dirty Business*, which is being distributed to unions in the U.S. and Canada. Demonstrations were held in many cities across the U.S. and in London at Grand Met headquarters. A picket line in Minneapolis was organized with help from UAW Local 879.

  The idea of workers in one local union taking on a corporate giant like Grand Met seems like David versus Goliath. But the campaign was taken up by the AFL-CIO-backed Coalition for Justice in the Maquiladoras and Free Trade. It is an active boycott with picket lines appearing around the U.S., Canada, and Britain.

Auto workers from three countries met in Mexico City in October 1990.

actions, to help set up worker-to-worker contacts, and to work with its counterparts, the Action Canada Network and the Mexican Action Network on Free Trade. The network can also educate the public through media appearances and releases, tours of union activists from the various countries, and international conferences.

To get on the network's mailing list, see chapter 12.

3. **Trinational conferences**, or binational ones, go a long way toward breaking down barriers and reversing old ways of thinking. In the last five years such conferences have been organized by Mujer a Mujer/Woman to Woman, Transnationals Information Exchange, American Labor Education Center, the Mexican Action Network on Free Trade, Action Canada Network, and others.

TRINATIONAL ALTERNATIVE

In October 1991, representatives from the Canadian, Mexican, and U.S. governments met in Zacatecas, Mexico to negotiate the NAFTA. Over 200 representatives from labor, agricultural, social, and political organizations in the three countries met in Zacatecas at the same time to hold their own alternative negotiations.

The meeting was hosted by the Mexican Action Network and drew broad participation from other Mexican opposition groups: top leaders of the PRD, PRT, and the right-wing PAN (National Action Party).

The conference issued a statement: citizens in the U.S., Mexico, and Canada must organize for a "development agreement" rather than a free trade agreement. "We insist that trade be part of a strategy of continental development that guarantees the distribution of wealth, the elevation of living standards, and the self-determination of our peoples," the declaration said.

For American unionists, getting to know their Mexican counterparts personally can make all the difference between an abstract commitment to solidarity and a zeal to make it happen in their own workplaces. Brad Markell, a member of UAW Local 1776, attended the trinational auto workers conference described above. "I was able to gain direct knowledge about the conditions and attitudes of the Mexican workers," said Markell, "and I learned that they're just as concerned as we are about the companies pitting Mexican workers against U.S. workers."

Because of cost (not many Mexican unionists can afford to come to the U.S.), it makes sense to hold such conferences in Mexico. Given that many general conferences have already taken place, it is probably the best use of resources now for unions to concentrate on more specific meetings, by industry or by company.

4. **Industry-wide or corporation-wide networks** are a necessity now that industry is internationally integrated. The trinational auto network described above is one example.

Contacts in other countries can be made through TIE, Labor Notes, the national grassroots network, or other organizations listed in chapter 12. To find whether your company has operations in Canada or Mexico, look in *Moody's Manual, Dun and Bradstreet's Million Dollar Directory,* or *Standard & Poor's Register of Corporations,* available in most public libraries. The company's annual reports also have information about activities abroad. (See *A Troublemaker's Handbook* for more on researching your employer.)

Today's electronic communication makes such networks far more feasible than they were even ten years ago. See chapter 12 for information on the PeaceNet computer network.

As first steps, such networks can exchange information on wages, benefits, working conditions, and company strategies; develop com-

---

NOT ONE BIG UNION

Some attempts at union coordination across borders have turned out poorly. Prior to 1985, for example, the United Auto Workers union included both American and Canadian workers and bargained for both with the Big Three. For most of its history, the UAW did a decent job of maintaining parity. But during the 1980s, the UAW leadership adopted a policy of concessions and labor-management cooperation. The Canadians didn't go along; pressure from American leaders to conform was taken as both an insult to Canadian autonomy and a barrier to successful bargaining. In 1985, the Canadians left to form the Canadian Auto Workers. Several other Canadian sections of U.S-dominated unions also formed their own unions during the 1980s.

We are not proposing common unions for workers in the U.S., Canada, and Mexico. Different national traditions of unionism and approaches to bargaining should not be jammed into one mold. Nor would it be right for the workers of one nation, simply by virtue of their numbers, always to dominate the union. Genuine internationalism requires respect for national sensibilities.

Jack Hedrick of UAW Local 249 leaflets a bus of Cuautitlán workers.

mon demands; and monitor labor and human rights conditions. As the networks develop they can support demands of lower-paid workers; conduct protest actions throughout the corporation's workplaces; and pressure the unions in their industry to move toward coordinated bargaining.

The first trinational action by unionists in the U.S., Mexico, and Canada was the January 8, 1991, Ford Workers Justice Day described earlier. The black commemorative ribbons were printed by the CAW, but worn in plants in all three countries. A similar black sticker was distributed by the UAW New Directions Movement in several plants in the U.S.

International networks need not be limited to workers in large corporations. Teachers in the U.S. and Mexico, for example, have already established contact. The Mexican union representing elementary teachers (SNTE) is working with the United Teachers of Los Angeles to establish sister schools.

5. **Internationally coordinated bargaining** within the same multinational corporation should be the next step. Such bargaining should involve all relevant unions from each country. The goal would not be a single contract or even identical contracts. Each national union or coalition of unions would be responsible for its own agreement.

Coordinated bargaining could begin as a joint effort to harmonize wages and conditions upward through mutual support and constant consultation. It could move toward genuine international bargaining over time as trust developed among the unions. This goal is already being pursued by unions in Europe in preparation for the European Single Market that will take effect in 1992; the steps made by FLOC and SNTOAC are another example.

Direct action—demonstrations, slowdowns or strikes—must be part of the arsenal in this strategy. To back up such actions, unions should set up an International Strike and Action Fund.

6. In many cases, it will be necessary to **change our unions** to get them in shape for international solidarity. The barriers are many. For example, some union leaders are committed to close labor-management cooperation; they may be unwilling to confront their corporate collaborators on behalf of foreign workers. Also, many AFL-CIO unions are still committed to a cold war view of foreign policy that does not lend itself to genuine internationalism.

Therefore, another step is to develop a common trend within the unions of the three countries, to fight for member-controlled, militant unions throughout the continent. Each nation has progressive and conservative, democratic and bureaucratic, militant and business-oriented unions. In some unions, reform movements exist. The activists in these various movements have a great deal in common and much to learn from one another.

CORPORATE WEAK POINTS

Dealing with multi-billion-dollar multinational corporations is no simple task. Often the power to alter their decisions seems beyond our reach. Yet, as organizations and networks dedicated to the solidarity strategy grow, the possibilities for powerful action will grow as well. Starting with symbolic events or pressure activities, it will be possible to move toward actions that carry more force. As unions and judo artists have long known, the proper force applied to weak points can yield results.

Corporations have more weak points than it first appears. Here are a few:

1. Today's corporations are deep in debt from financing their global empires. A corporate campaign against their creditors (banks, insurance companies) can sometimes make a difference. This was important in FLOC's 1986 contract victory at Campbell.
2. Most corporations are guilty of civil rights abuses or environmental violations; these create the opportunity for coalitions with other movements. The Oil, Chemical and Atomic Workers, for example, allied with environmentalists to stop the German multinational BASF's union busting in Louisiana. (This approach is described in detail in *A Troublemaker's Handbook*.)
3. Nowadays unions hear constantly that competition from foreign companies has put the union movement on the ropes. But competition is a two-edged sword. Traditionally, competition is the weak point of the company, not the union.

Competition is what makes the strike an effective weapon. A

strike means loss of production and thus loss of market share to competitors. With the fight over market shares sharper than ever today, it is in management's interest to settle a strike quickly or avoid it altogether.

4. The management-by-stress production system, integrated continent-wide, has its own weak points. Spreading out production into many different factories through outsourcing creates a growing number of points of vulnerability. Each plant in the stream of production is dependent on the one before. An interruption in production at any point upstream will eventually disrupt final assembly. And because the MBS system is linked on a just-in-time basis, any job action is felt downstream very quickly.

The German metalworkers union I.G. Metall used this approach in their 1985 strike for a shorter work week. By striking only a few plants in Germany, they closed down much of the metalworking industry there, as well as plants as far away as Spain. Non-striking workers collected unemployment insurance.

The UAW used this sort of link in 1988 when it discovered that Chrysler planned to sell off its Acustar parts division. The UAW threatened to conduct legal health and safety strikes in certain key plants. Chrysler, fearful of losing market share, backed off the sale. Here, integration and competition worked together for the union.

These corporate weak points could be powerful weapons for international networks of local unions. Ironically, the leaner the production system and the more intense the struggle for market shares, the more powerful is labor's leverage. This approach also has the advantage of not placing the burden of struggle too heavily on any one group. The action can move from one place to another and still affect the tightly integrated system.

POLITICAL ACTION

We need to put the fear of the people into the legislature.
—Bernice Zickwolf, President, CWA Local 1039, May 1991

The "new world order" of continental integration means that the labor movement needs new politics. Routine lobbying and the "write your Senators and Congressman" approach are not working. The bipartisan support for free trade shows why the labor movement needs to form its own independent party.

The leading Democrats in Congress are as committed to the free trade agenda as George Bush himself. It was after all, Richard Gephardt and Lloyd Bentsen who helped push free trade onto the fast track.

The situation is the same on other issues: corporate money and ideas reign. Several Democrats were found on or over the edge of Congressional ethics in the savings and loan scandal. Democrats lent their votes to breaking the April 1991 strike of 230,000 railroad workers. In state after state, Democrats, often elected with labor backing, have joined Republicans in imposing disastrous budget cuts on education and critical social programs.

The result of this bipartisan pro-business consensus is that the majority of people don't vote—less than half in presidential elections, less than a third in most Congressional or state-level elections. The voters are increasingly the rich and the upper middle classes. A majority of working people form the party of the non-voters, disaffected from a politics that offers them no hope.

It doesn't have to be this way. Canadians have reacted to their national elite's corporate agenda by sweeping the labor-based New Democratic Party (NDP) into office in three provinces and the Yukon Territory. The NDP now governs 52% of the Canadian population.

In the U.S., polls conducted in locals of the UAW, OCAW, AFSCME, and among local officials in Wisconsin showed a majority saying that now is the time to make a break from the Democrats and organize a new party of working people.

Indeed, 1991 was the year that independent politics returned to the vocabulary of the labor movement:

- Tony Mazzocchi, former secretary-treasurer of the Oil, Chemical, and Atomic Workers, launched Labor Party Advocates—a membership organization dedicated to promoting the idea of a labor party.

- Independent democratic socialist Bernie Sanders went to Congress from Vermont with the backing of the state's labor movement.

- Communications Workers locals in New Jersey, made up of public employees, put forth their own independent candidates in the 1991 elections, forcing the state government to back off some of its more blatant anti-labor moves.

American workers need their own party to ally with the NDP in Canada and with reform forces in Mexico. In the long run, the victory of a new politics in the three nations of North America can allow working people to renegotiate the entire basis of economic integration—for one that is based on national sovereignty, ecologically sound development, and the satisfaction of human needs.

MATT WITT/Impact Visuals

January 26, 1990: Cuautitlán workers protest murder of Cleto Nigmo.

CHAPTER 9

Auto Workers and Free Trade

In response to overseas competition, the U.S. automobile industry undertook a dramatic restructuring over the last 10 years. It included the decentralization of production through outsourcing, on the one hand, and workplace "flexibility" through management-by-stress, on the other.

By removing all barriers to trade and investment, the North American Free Trade Agreement will accelerate these trends. Management's plans for the 1990s include both outsourcing of a broader range of parts to Mexico, and relocation of most small car and small truck production to northern Mexico.

RESTRUCTURING: THE 1980s

Altogether 208,000 U.S. auto jobs, union and non-union, were lost between 1978 and 1990. Over 80% of this loss occurred in the assembly and core components (e.g., engines, transmissions, high-volume stampings) sector of the industry. It was caused by productivity increases in assembly plants (over 14% a year between 1985 and 1989) and by outsourcing of parts abroad.

U.S. AUTO PRODUCTION WORKERS

Year	Total	Assembly	Core Components	Other Parts
1978	1,032,000	416,000	366,000	250,000
1989	885,000	328,000	335,000	222,000
1990	824,000	292,000	318,000	214,000
Change	-208,000	-124,000	-48,000	-36,000

Source: Stephen Herzenberg, "The North American Auto Industry at the Onset of Continental Free Trade Negotiations," Economic Discussion Paper 38, U.S. Department of Labor, 1991.

Until the late 1970s, the Big Three produced their core parts in-house and bought about 50% of the value of a car from suppliers. Since then the industry has moved to "vertical disintegration," outsourcing more of the content of cars and trucks.

At the same time, the Big Three (and the transplants) drastically reduced the number of their first-line suppliers, in order to gain greater control over costs, quality, and delivery time. Ford, for example, reduced its first-line suppliers in the U.S. and Canada from 20,000 in 1985 to 6,000 in 1989. These first-line suppliers buy their parts from thousands of smaller firms whose costs and delivery they in turn attempt to control.

This reorganization presents new problems for the United Auto Workers in at least three ways. First, the big companies pressure their suppliers for price reductions. In 1991, GM asked its suppliers for price cuts totalling 7% over three years and Ford for as much as 25% over five years. This puts pressure on supplier wages.

Second, these first-line suppliers, in turn, seek lowest-cost components from smaller producers—often abroad or in the South, and increasingly non-union. This has led the UAW's share of parts jobs to drop from 82% in 1976-77 to 58% in 1987-88. Union coverage in non-Big Three parts plants fell from 59% to 24%.

Finally, wages tend to drop with each tier, creating a widening gap between workers in the assembly companies and in supplier firms. In 1978 real wages in the parts sector were 90% of those in the assembly and core components sector; by 1990 only 76%.

INTERNATIONAL "DISINTEGRATION"

In the 1980s, companies turned more and more to outsourcing in Asia and Latin America. The percentage of imported auto parts (not including parts from Canada) rose from 6% of the U.S. market in 1982 to 16% in 1987. In the early stages, South Korea, Taiwan, Singapore, Brazil, and Mexico were all contenders. By the end of the 1980s, Mexico had pulled ahead of the pack. Mexico's export-oriented parts industry grew by about 82,000 jobs over the decade. At the same time, 84,000 jobs in core components and other parts (Big Three, transplants, and independent suppliers) were lost in the U.S.

MAQUILADORA AUTO EMPLOYMENT IN MEXICO

1980	1981	1982	1983	1984	1985	1986	1987	1989
7,500	10,999	12,288	19,594	29,170	40,085	49,048	59,278	93,278

Source: Harley Shaiken, *Mexico in the Global Economy*, University of California, San Diego, 1990.

NON-MAQUILA EMPLOYMENT OF MAJOR AUTO ASSEMBLY FIRMS IN MEXICO

1960	1981	1985	1986	1987
5,610	52,951	49,747	47,514	44,134

Source: Herzenberg, 1991.

TOTAL BIG THREE EMPLOYMENT IN MEXICO

	1980	1985	1988	1989
GM	6,463	10,347	47,846	54,340
Chrysler	7,928	10,483	19,665	NA
Ford	7,819	8,629	12,734	17,203
Total	22,210	29,459	80,245	NA

Source: Centro de Investigación Laboral Asesoría Sindical (CILAS), September 1991, Mexico City; Herzenberg, 1991.

By the end of the 1980s Mexico lagged behind only Canada and Japan as the largest exporter of auto parts to the U.S. Now it is also becoming a site of small car production for the U.S. market. Mexican car exports rose from 14,428 in 1981 to 195,994 in 1989. Some estimate that Mexico could export as many as 500,000 cars annually to the U.S. by 1994. Light truck exports have been discouraged by a 25% tariff—which will be removed by the NAFTA.

THE COMING REORGANIZATION

U.S. negotiators in the NAFTA talks have demanded the immediate removal of barriers to automotive exports from Mexico. Thus, unlike in some other industries, in auto there will be no phasing in of free trade. The speed at which production moves to Mexico will depend only on construction and launch times for different types of plants, the availability of investment funds, competitive pressures, and overall market conditions.

According to a recent study at the Massachusetts Institute of Technology (MIT), two types of production will move to Mexico in the 1990s: small cars and trucks, and core components such as engines and drive trains.

Ford began this trend, building Escorts and Tracers at an ultramodern plant in Hermosillo. Sixty percent of Mexican imports in the 1980s were 4-cylinder models. Larger cars and vans will remain in the U.S., the MIT study predicts, presumably because of their higher profitability.

Compact and subcompact cars composed about 30% of U.S.- and Canadian-made cars sold in the U.S. in recent years. Thus the shift to Mexico could eliminate up to 75,000 U.S. jobs in the assembly sector and more in the parts sector. These losses would be concentrated in the Big Three and in the Midwest.

The Department of Commerce expects the U.S. market to top off at 10.5 million cars and 4.8 million light trucks a year in the mid-1990s. The Mexican market is expected to grow only slightly, and Canadian consumption not at all. This means that the shift to production in Mexico occurs in a fixed North American market.

THE FATE OF MEXICO'S DOMESTIC AUTO INDUSTRY

Long before the Big Three began building maquila parts plants there for export, Mexico had a domestic industry producing for home consumption. Most of it was located in central Mexico.

Now this domestic industry is declining, both because of the shift to export production and because, under the government's austerity program, fewer Mexicans can afford cars. As the table on page 60 shows, non-maquila auto employment fell by nearly 9,000 jobs from 1981 to 1987. Workers also saw their wages and benefits decline, from $5.27 an hour in 1982 to $2.45 in 1987.

All of the growth in passenger car production during the 1980s was in exports. They grew from nothing in 1981 to 41% of all car production in 1990. But wages in most export-oriented plants located in the north were significantly below those in the older plants of central Mexico.

A major shift of small car production to Mexico would involve massive investment. As the director of Ford of Mexico, quoted in *UAW Ammo*, put it: "We're going to see investment pour in here. The dollar numbers are going to make people's heads spin."

Shifting a major portion of assembly work to Mexico does create problems for the auto companies, however. For one thing, it costs much more to build an integrated assembly plant than most parts plants. And, with Japanese automakers also moving into North America, there is the risk of re-creating overcapacity. In this context, even a slight slump in the U.S. market could render such a large investment in Mexico unprofitable.

All of these risks and costs are justifiable from a business point of view if the returns continue to be of the magnitude of those at Hermosillo described in chapter 2. Without a clear upward trend in Mexican wages and vigorous opposition from the unions in the U.S. and Canada, the MIT scenario or something close to it will be the future of the North American auto industry.

OUTSOURCING ESCALATES

The types of parts outsourced to Mexico will expand in the 1990s. In the 1980s Mexico's largest exports were electrical, rubber, and plastic components and accessories—low-cost, labor-intensive parts. Before the flight to Mexico, most of these had been produced in smaller plants in the U.S. paying well below the Big Three level.

Now the auto companies will begin to outsource the core components: engines, generators, brakes, wheels, and transmissions. Mexico already has some experience producing these parts. This time, the jobs lost will be high-paid ones, both at suppliers and in the Big Three itself.

The companies face less risk than in building new assembly plants, because the construction of most parts plants costs less. In addition, unionism remains marginal in the maquila parts plants. So far, the Big Three experience with maquilas has been positive from management's point of view.

Analysts Stephen Herzenberg and Harley Shaiken estimate that by the year 2000, workers in the U.S. will lose 270,000 auto jobs. Almost 80% of this loss will occur in assembly and core components—primarily in the Big Three.

NAFTA WILL REDUCE SOME IMPORTS

The "rules of origin" in the NAFTA will tend to reduce imports from outside of North America somewhat. Asian, European, and Brazilian parts accounted for 71% of non-Canadian imports into the U.S. by the late 1980s, or 11.3% of total U.S. sales in the eight major parts groups. A reduction of these non-North American imports by one-third could lead to the creation of 20,000 parts jobs in North America.

Even if all of these new jobs ended up in Mexico, this would not lead to any net loss in the U.S. or Canada, since this production would simply be replacing imports. More likely, given the tendency of the Japanese to build parts plants in all three countries (partly because of just-in-time), some of the jobs would end up in the U.S., in non-union plants.

UNION RESPONSE

During the 1980s, the United Auto Workers accepted and then embraced the Big Three's reorganization of the industry along management-by-stress lines. Concern for the profitability of the Big Three has led the UAW leadership to collaborate in the whole outsourcing, "lean" strategy that has already cost tens of thousands of jobs. This has made the UAW leadership unwilling to intervene on behalf of embattled Mexican auto workers.

A new vision of union functioning from top to bottom is needed for this era, one that is actively internationalist. Its goal must be industry stability and job security in all three countries:

- While opposing outsourcing, the UAW should support saving Canada's and Mexico's domestic auto industries.

- UAW leaders should take the lead in a trinational campaign for the shorter work week. This is particularly important for Mexican auto workers, who often work 48 hours a week. Shortening and equalizing the work week within North America would save thousands of jobs in all three countries.

- The major goal of the unions in all three countries should be to raise Mexican wages.

The auto companies have achieved more than most employers in winning deregulation and flexibility, all the way from the shop floor to the world market. In doing so, they have brought American, Canadian, and Mexican auto workers into internationally integrated production systems, often under the roof of a common employer. Auto workers can turn their new shared condition into organized trinational networks, such as were initiated at the 1991 North American Auto Workers Conference. Over time, these networks can exploit the weak points in the new "lean" system to re-establish union power in the automobile industry.

CHAPTER 10

Telecommunications Goes Global

Only a few years ago, the very idea of trade in telecommunications seemed implausible. Telephone service was controlled by national publicly owned or regulated monopolies in most countries. Competition was nonexistent in international traffic, where rates were set nationally and not by any market. In the U.S., privately-owned AT&T and its Bell System operating companies enjoyed guaranteed profit margins under state regulation.

But few industries have changed as rapidly under deregulation as telecommunications. Since the government broke up the Bell system in 1984, competition, internationalization, and new technology have drastically changed the nature of work, services offered, rates charged, and company organization. These in turn have brought challenges to the unions in this industry, above all to the Communications Workers of America.

The NAFTA will affect telecommunications workers by accelerating three trends: 1) internationalization and diversification of AT&T and the regional Bell operating companies, 2) changes in the traditional rate structure, and 3) relocation of operations.

DEREGULATION, 1984-90

The breakup of the Bell System in 1984 produced eight separate companies: AT&T, handling long distance and manufacturing a full range of telecommunications equipment, and seven regional Bell operating companies (RBOCs) or "Baby Bells", made up of 22 subsidiaries. Ameritech, for example, controls the state Bell companies in Michigan, Ohio, Indiana, Illinois, and Wisconsin. AT&T absorbed Western Electric, which made telephone equipment. The RBOCs now compete with one another and with AT&T in selling home telephone equipment.

Under the old conditions, the CWA had established national bargaining. During the 1970s and early 1980s, average hourly wages rose by 10% a year. After 1984, the CWA and other unions had to bargain with eight major units and more subsidiaries.

Although the industry grew, new technology eliminated jobs at a faster rate. About 80,000 non-supervisory jobs were lost between 1983 and 1990. Union membership at AT&T dropped from 70% in 1984 to 50% in 1990. Under these circumstances, hourly wages rose by an annual average of only 2.6%—much less than inflation.

Job loss in telecommunications services is particularly troublesome because it is one of the areas in which women and minority workers have been able to find unionized jobs. About 50% of the workforce is women, while African American and Latino workers make up 18%.

Deregulation within the U.S. has been hard enough on telephone workers. Free trade will introduce still more competition, this time across borders.

GLOBAL AND DIVERSE: NOT JUST THE PHONE COMPANY ANY MORE

Phone companies are branching out, both into new businesses and into new countries. Diversification plus internationalization spells a loss in union power, as the companies draw more of their revenues from outside the unions' traditional strongholds.

The rise of nonunion long distance outfits like MCI, U.S. Sprint, and Allnet, along with independent wire and wireless services (cellular, cable TV, electronic mail), has increased competition and reduced the union presence in the industry. Most RBOCs have

Ojos de Lucha

created new (usually nonunion) subsidiaries offering these new services. Other companies have merged, for example, GTE with Telcom and AT&T with NCR (formerly National Cash Register, now a computer company).

The AT&T-NCR merger illustrates the problems the unions in this industry face. According to a CWA report, this $8.9 billion merger will reduce the proportion of AT&T's union employees in the U.S. from 50% to 46%. In addition, it will make AT&T a real multinational firm. Its international revenues will increase from 15% to 22% of total revenues and its overseas employees will increase from 7% to 14%.

As in so many industries, internationalization in telecommunications was already well under way before the the North American Free Trade Agreement, but the NAFTA will accelerate the process. The most obvious aspect is the rise of international telephone traffic. In terms of revenues, international traffic from and to the

U.S. has grown at a rate of about 18% a year recently, compared to about 5% for domestic traffic. International traffic is projected to provide 5% of total revenues by the end of 1991 (double the percentage of 20 years ago). Although it remains small in comparison to domestic traffic, it is more profitable.

The phone companies are also investing abroad. AT&T increased its international presence through the merger with NCR and a number of overseas joint service agreements. Various RBOCs have bought cellular firms in Europe, Argentina, and Mexico. Ameritech and Bell Atlantic jointly purchased New Zealand's state-owned phone system for $2.4 billion.

Telefonicos de Mexico (TELMEX) was snapped up by Southwestern Bell, France Telecom, and a Mexican financial group when the government put it on the auction block. This deal turned Southwestern Bell into a multinational corporation. It gained the right, upheld in a U.S. court, to engage directly in long distance service—something the RBOCs were previously denied.

TELEPHONE RATES AND THE SQUEEZE ON WAGES

Historically, the delivery of telephone service to over 90% of U.S. households was made possible by a government-regulated rate structure. Higher long distance and international rates subsidized lower local rates. Since there was no serious competition, there was little pressure to lower long distance rates. Deregulation and the rise of competing long distance companies changed that.

As the big three long distance providers—AT&T, MCI, and U.S. Sprint—slug it out for market share, they lower long distance and international rates and offer special deals. The average cost of an international message unit, for example, fell by 55% from 1975 to 1988. This has in turn depressed profits in the RBOCs, who get 25% of their revenue from long distance access fees. To protect their profit rates they have attempted to chisel on wages and benefits. That is largely what lay behind the 1990 strike at NYNEX, the RBOC for New York and New England.

PROFITS AND WAGES AS PERCENTAGE OF REVENUES (SALES) 1986-90

Company	PROFITS			WAGES		
	1986	1990	Change	1986	1990	Change
Ameritech	25.8%	20.5%	-5.2%	24.9%	24.0%	-0.9%
Bell Atlantic	24.6%	21.2%	-3.4%	25.6%	22.6%	-3.0%
Bell South	30.2%	21.1%	-9.1%	24.5%	23.7%	-0.8%
NYNEX	22.2%	14.8%	-7.3%	26.6%	25.3%	-1.3%
Pacific Telesis	27.7%	22.9%	-4.8%	29.5%	31.0%	1.5%
So'west. Bell	27.8%	22.5%	-5.3%	31.1%	29.7%	-1.4%
U.S. West	25.0%	24.4%	-0.5%	26.4%	24.1%	-2.3%

Source: *CWA Information Industry Report*, August 1991.

WILL CONSUMERS BENEFIT FROM DECLINING RATES?

Until recently, local rates on private home service have been subsidized by higher rates for business customers and long distance calls. Competition, however, is forcing long distance rates down, and competition for business customers could bring down business rates as well. Some RBOCs are losing local business traffic as corporations use the new technology to create their own internal telephone systems. Sears now offers an alternative local phone service in some areas. With this kind of competition, in the near future phone companies are likely to give businesses a break and pass along costs to the individual or family consumer.

The common interest of consumers and workers lies in keeping home rates low and business rates higher. Joint pressure on public utility commissions, which still set rates in most states, is one way to keep home phone service affordable.

Competition for shares in the growing Mexican-U.S. market will tend to lower international rates (and thus RBOC income) even further. Both the long distance companies and the RBOCs will try to make their workers pay for these lost revenues through contract concessions.

WHIPSAWING AND THE RELOCATION OF SERVICES

Technological innovations have broken the link between the location of the telephone switching center and the delivery of service. Satellite, microwave, and fiber optic technologies have brought geographic flexibility to competing delivery companies and to businesses operating their own communications systems. For some time now businesses have been able to locate data processing computer centers overseas. Many corporations have used the same technology to develop their own internal "by-pass" systems. Some of these actually compete with local phone companies.

In a similar vein, a Bell Canada supervisor told two visiting Mexican telephone workers in May 1991 that excess Canadian traffic could be routed through Mexico and back into Canada. For automated traffic, this simply involves using satellite transmission to route through another switching center. In the U.S., operators have long been located at centers remote from the local exchange. There is no technological barrier to locating operators in another country. Only national regulation has prevented this to date, and the NAFTA will almost certainly take care of that. In fact, a small partly-owned subsidiary of Telmex in the Mexican state of Baja California is already offering alternative operator services to southern California.

AT&T has a new ground-to-satellite transmitting facility in

California that communicates with 12 similar facilities in the Pacific Rim. Under NAFTA, this facility could as easily be located in Mexico where it would cost less to build and operate. Using the instant connection allowed by this technology, switching-transmission centers could also be relocated to Mexico or other low-cost areas.

The ability to relocate work not only threatens jobs in the U.S. and Canada. It also opens the door to the kind of whipsawing already common in manufacturing. Mexican telephone wages are a fraction of those in the rest of North America.

THE UNIONS RESPOND

The major U.S. and Canadian unions in telecommunications services and equipment manufacturing have responded to these sweeping changes in the industry in a fairly aggressive manner. The CWA has used membership mobilizations in its last two contract fights. They have also taken international solidarity seriously.

In 1990, the CWA, Canadian Auto Workers (CAW), and Communications and Electrical Workers of Canada (CWC) formed an alliance to deal with the union-busting policies of Northern Telecom, an equipment manufacturer and subsidiary of Bell Canada. Northern Telecom had moved into the U.S. market in the 1980s to compete with AT&T. In the U.S., it is only 4% unionized, compared to 44% in Canada.

When the CWA struck one of Northern Telecom's U.S. facilities, the CWC and CAW gave them energetic support in Canada and the strike was settled favorably.

This alliance has continued with a campaign against Northern Telecom's covert surveillance of its workers. The alliance is also looking to unions in other countries, as Northern Telecom cuts deals with phone companies around the world, including TELMEX, to whom it sells automated operator equipment. As Richard Long of the CWC says, "NT will be moving into new markets and we will be there to influence the unions so they can have an influence over the products the company purchases. They can run, but they can't hide."

In December 1991, the CWA, the CWC, and the Mexican union STRM (Sindicato de Telefonistas de la Republica Mexicana) formed a permanent coalition. This coalition was all the more remarkable because the three unions didn't agree on the NAFTA. The Mexican union leadership supports the NAFTA, while the U.S. and Canadian unions oppose it. Their agreement focuses on strengthening the ability of each union to bargain; supporting joint mobilizations if there is a strike; and defending unions' and workers' rights in alliance with the international trade secretariats and other social movements in each country.

The STRM represents something new in the Mexican labor movement. It is not part of the main labor federation, the CTM, but is one of several unions that founded the new Federation of Goods and Service Workers (FESEBES) in 1990.

STRM and the other FESEBES affiliates are regarded as free of CTM-style corruption. But at the same time, STRM is dedicated to modernization of the type pushed by President Carlos Salinas. STRM's General Secretary, Francisco Hernandez Juarez, is a personal friend of the President. The union supported the government's sale of TELMEX and also technological change in order to make the company more marketable. It has been willing to make concessions on working conditions, subcontracting, and even job security. About 10,000 or 80% of all TELMEX operators will lose their jobs as Northern Telecom's digital TOPS system replaces older Ericson switchboards. For technicians, modernization has already meant job loss as more maintenance work is subcontracted.

These changes have produced an opposition movement within STRM. In August 1991, in Cuernavaca, about 50 Mexican activists from the democratic movement within the STRM and from a smaller union in Baja California met, along with representatives from the U.S. and Canada.

Conference participants insisted they were not opposed to technological change, but pointed out that management often uses innovation as an excuse for speedup, more shift work, new incentive pay schemes, forced relocations, craft deskilling, part-timing, and pay cuts. They agreed that the relevant question for telecommunications unionists was whether modernization would benefit workers and individual or family users, or only the corporations that own and use the telecommunications companies.

CHAPTER 11

Airline Workers In The "Open Skies"

"Open skies." The term conjures up notions of freedom, broad vistas, sunshine. Who could object? Open skies—the international deregulation of air transportation—is the airlines' version of free trade. It will in fact bring more freedom—for airline owners. For airline workers, free trade will bring layoffs, lower wages, and lower safety standards. For the flying public, it means less service to cities off the beaten (profitable) track, and, again, lower safety standards.

Most of the negotiations over open skies are not a part of the North American Free Trade Agreement itself (NAFTA). But these talks are heavily influenced by the whole free trade atmosphere and by big changes which are already happening in the industry:

1. *Deregulation*, which began in the U.S. in 1978 and spread to Canada and Mexico in the late 1980s. Government-owned airlines there were privatized.
2. *Globalization*. Domestic airlines are moving into international routes, more airlines are competing for prime international routes (the Pacific Rim, Europe), and many are turning to international mergers or alliances.

We'll look briefly at these forces which are paving the runway for open skies and then at how open skies could affect airline workers.

DEREGULATION AND GLOBALIZATION

When airlines are deregulated, all sorts of matters are no longer under government control: fares, route and gate ownership, entry to the industry, types of equipment ownership (leasing vs. direct ownership), and location of maintenance within the country. Deregulation has been disastrous for workers, causing mergers, buy-ups, and bankruptcies. The 1980s saw wage cuts in almost all occupations, the hiring of new workers at significantly lower (B-scale) wage rates, the erosion of work and scheduling rules, and the decline of job security. (For a fuller discussion, see "Airlines: A Two-Tier Industry in Trouble," listed in chapter 12.)

As more and more corporations have gone multinational, international air traffic has grown faster than domestic. Measured in ton miles, from 1981 to 1990 the international traffic of all the world's commercial airlines grew by 36%, compared to 20% for domestic. International passenger revenue miles (PRM) flown by U.S. majors grew by 145%, while domestic PRM grew by only 89%.

Privatization is another globalizing force. Most national airlines in Europe, Asia, and South America, as well as in Canada and Mexico, have been privatized, opening them to investment by other countries' carriers.

Air transport is governed by an international agreement called the Chicago Convention of 1944. Many aspects of airline operations are also written into various countries' laws. But as more governments have deregulated airlines, national laws have been modified or bent.

Today's major carriers are pushing the limits of this legal framework and establishing new precedents. Among these are various partnerships, ranging from "interlining" computer reservation systems to ownership stakes in overseas carriers.

"No, no! I'm sure you're not mine!"

More than 100 airlines now have such arrangements. SAS, based in Scandinavia, has agreements with eleven airlines and part ownership in three (including Continental, where only the flight attendants have a union). Delta, nonunion except for its pilots, has a partnership with Swissair and Air Singapore in which each carrier owns 5% of the other.

These arrangements raise the possibility that aspects of airline operation that are now carried out strictly in the home country could be internationalized. James Ott, a senior editor of *Aviation Week and Space Technology*, writes:

> Alliances that begin with a beneficial exchange of traffic can ...develop...programs to maintain and operate like aircraft, to train personnel, or to jointly buy supplies. (November 26, 1990)

This could have far-reaching implications for both ground and cabin personnel, such as cabotage (rhymes with "sabotage"). This means an airline of one nation carrying passengers within another nation. Most countries have resisted cabotage, because the Chicago Convention strongly implies that if a country grants it to one other nation, it must grant it to all. A foot in the cabin door can occur de facto, however, through a partnership arrangement.

For example, All Nippon Airways has a 9% stake in Austrian Air.

They fly a joint Tokyo-to-Vienna flight on which Austrian's aircraft is staffed by All Nippon personnel. In effect, small Austrian, which ranks 63rd among the top 100 airlines, has opened the European door for All Nippon, a giant that ranks ninth in the world.

What is unique in this agreement is that the crew of one nation's airline is allowed to work in the equipment of another. Given the differences in wage levels between countries, this sort of arrangement almost automatically introduces a B-scale for cabin crews working on the same equipment.

Ott also speculates that such agreements will lead to "joint ventures for aircraft maintenance"—large, strategically located maintenance centers. In fact, just such a facility is being built by a Hong Kong-Mexican consortium adjacent to Tijuana International airport. It will open for business in 1993. This is an international version of the hub system that could cost thousands of airframe and power technician (mechanic) jobs in higher wage countries. According to the AFL-CIO, this center can legally service U.S. carriers.

OPEN SKIES AND THE NAFTA

Secretary of Transportation Samuel Skinner says that the U.S. is "stripping away the artificial constraints of bilateral agreements" and pushing for an open skies policy. He favors doing away with the Chicago Convention, and wants to open up all national markets to all airlines. For now, however, the carriers and the government must still act in the framework of the Chicago Convention, so they are whittling it away piecemeal.

The Reagan and Bush Administrations have pushed for cabotage, as has Democrat James Oberstar, chair of the House Public Works Aviation Subcommittee. And recently the U.S. changed its restriction on foreign ownership of airlines from a 25% maximum of voting stock to 49%. Negotiations are under way with Canada for a bilateral open skies agreement.

The NAFTA will place enormous pressure on all three North American countries to negotiate open skies. Even aside from the pressures of harmonization, the geographic restructuring of industry will move a great deal of business travel southward. It was, in fact, the U.S.-Canada FTA that changed the Canadian government's previous opposition to open skies and cabotage. The major U.S. carriers and Air Canada want cabotage to break into each other's markets. Of the majors, only smaller Canadian Air still opposes cabotage.

The Canadians note that as their air traffic shifts from its older east-west direction to north-south service to the U.S., it is the big U.S. carriers that are getting the business. The Canadian Union of Public Employees (CUPE), which represents flight attendants on Canada's major airlines and subsidiaries, estimates that 8,800 jobs were lost there between January 1989 (the implementation of the

FTA) and February 1991. Seven airlines were bought out and another seven went bankrupt. Executives say that Canada's two major carriers, Air Canada and Canadian Air, will have to merge to survive in this new market. This would cost another 10,000 jobs, CUPE estimates.

In Europe, where the airlines are preparing for the European Single Market in 1992, the story is the same. International competition is causing job loss in spite of the growth of international traffic. In 1990 and 1991, British Airways laid off over 4,000 workers, SAS cut 3,500, KLM let 1,100 go, Alitalia another 2,500, and Air Europe went belly-up. The International Transport Workers Federation (the trade secretariat of transport unions around the world) estimates that another 25,000 airline jobs in the U.S. and Europe will be lost to international competition in the next few years.

Mexico has already gone through the first phase of preparing for international competition. Both Aeromexico and Mexicana were privatized in the late 1980s. Both airlines took the opportunity to cut their workforces, reduce pay, and eliminate work rules. Aeromexico fired all 1,450 of its flight attendants, rehiring only 800, without regard to seniority. At their U.S. operations they replaced their IAM mechanics with a nonunion contractor.

The shift of plants and services to Mexico under the NAFTA will increase air traffic to and within Mexico and decrease traffic in previously industrial areas of the U.S. and Canada. This will cost some U.S. and Canadian jobs, and also make the Mexican market (flown largely by U.S., Canadian, and Japanese executives) a bigger plum.

But even with their lower labor costs, Mexico's two airlines are unlikely to survive continental competition without merging or being integrated into a U.S. major. This is not so unlikely, since two of the chief owners of Mexicana—Chase Manhattan Bank and Drexel Burnham Lambert—also own shares in United and other U.S. carriers. Thus a new wave of mergers and consolidations is likely.

Most analysts predict that at the end of the shakeout, we will see a small number of international megacarriers, because of the economies of scale that will be needed to compete. This alone will cost jobs. Furthermore, it will create new C- and D-scales, not only between nations, but *within* the merged megacarriers flying the open skies of North America. This makes collective bargaining even more problematic than it has been under national deregulation. But there is more.

LORENZO IN THE SKY WITH DOLLARS?

With open skies comes the possibility of the "flag of convenience." Practiced in maritime transportation, this allows a U.S.-owned carrier to register, crew, and maintain its ships in another country where wages are lower and regulations more lax.

Panama is one of the more popular flags of convenience. Richard Nolan, president of CUPE's airline division, presented the following scenario to Congress:

> Consider this: what if Frank Lorenzo takes his $30 million (when it is freed by the courts) and sets up Texas Air II as an offshore airline in Mexico or elsewhere....How will you be able to regulate the safety of these new Flag of Convenience air carriers, who will be able to freely fly the whole North American internal market?

More likely than Lorenzo are Chase Manhattan, Drexel Burnham, United, Delta, or American—or perhaps even British Airways or All Nippon. But the idea is the same. Cabin crews can be staffed by lower-paid Mexican workers. Maintenance centers located at lower-cost sites in Mexico can serve much of the continental fleet.

The point is not that Mexican workers don't deserve jobs in tomorrow's North American airline industry or that they can't do the work as well as anyone else. Mexican flight attendants already have to speak English to get the job. Furthermore, they are tested and licensed by the government in safety matters—something U.S. flight attendant unions have long wanted. As the experience of the auto industry shows, Mexican workers can perform high tech jobs at world class standards.

What is at stake are lower, "harmonized" safety standards and enforcement, on the one hand, and job security, decent wages and conditions in all three nations, on the other. There should be no discrimination on the grounds of national origin where carriers operate internationally. There must be uniformity of training and licensing requirements, wages, benefits, and conditions, within any carrier—no A- and B-scales by nationality. This means fighting for the highest standards through both collective bargaining and political action.

UNIONISM WITHOUT BORDERS FOR AN INDUSTRY WITHOUT BORDERS

American airline workers face a number of barriers to international solidarity. First, while there is always talk about greater solidarity among airline unions, so far a go-it-alone attitude prevails.

In addition, the legal protections for airline bargaining are deteriorating. Most airline contracts contain "labor protective provisions," which furnish some job security if the airline is merged or bought out. But for some time now, the Department of Transportation has refused to enforce these clauses.

A court ruling during the Eastern strike undermined the right to secondary boycotts or sympathy strikes, which are legal under the Railway Labor Act. Finally, a recent U.S. Court of Appeals decision took away contract protections on some international flights. A flight attendant, for example, who is covered by a union contract on domestic flights or even overseas flights to a single point, loses that protection if the plane stops in a third country or stops twice overseas. Thus, unionized workers on a flight stopping twice in Mexico or Canada would have no contractual protection while on that wing of the flight.

Open skies require an open and international approach from airline unions. Long-standing national laws that restrict staffing by citizenship will no longer do the trick in the new context. Airline workers need legislation giving unions the right to bargain agreements covering anywhere an airline employee goes on the job. Similar laws will be needed in Canada and Mexico to make sure everyone receives equal protection. Unified pressure for such laws, along with efforts to upwardly harmonize union contracts, could be a campaign around which the unions in North America learn to cooperate.

In any case, the unions representing airline workers in the three countries need to meet and determine an overall strategy. So far, with the exception of some meetings between ALPA and CALPA (Canadian Air Line Pilots Association), there is not much talk of such a step.

There is much that can be done without waiting for the top leadership of the unions to act. Cross-border, joint activity could be initiated by local union trinational solidarity committees.

Suppose, for example, that U.S. and Canadian unionists had been organized to lend support to Mexican airline workers when they resisted first the privatization of their airlines, and then the wage and rule cuts that followed. Many Mexican unionists were fired for resisting, and no one in North America came to their aid. At the same time, Mexicana dumped its IAM-organized mechanics in the U.S. for a subcontractor. An international labor rights campaign in support of both groups of workers might have helped them hold on to what they had. Instead, the AFL-CIO put Mexicana on its official boycott list for dumping the IAM members, but didn't say a thing about the Mexican workers.

Open skies are coming. The question is, will airline workers and their unions be prepared?

CHAPTER 12
Resources

ORGANIZER'S PACKET

• Contains practical advice on launching solidarity work. Includes a directory of organizations involved in trinational solidarity work in the U.S., Canada, and Mexico; a step-by-step guide to starting a local union international solidarity committee; testimony from workers whos jobs were exported to Mexico; a guide to finding your employer's holdings in Mexico and to connecting with unions there; advice on early detection of your employer's plans to move out work; and photos and information on living and working conditions in Mexico. $3 plus $2 postage. Labor Notes, 7435 Michigan Avenue, Detroit, MI 48210. 313-842-6262.

VIDEOS

• "$4 a Day? No Way! Joining Hands Across Borders," 1991. Focuses on Mexican workers' struggles, trinational solidarity, and runaway corporations. $30 for 1/2" VHS. 19 minutes. American Labor Education Center (ALEC), 2000 P St. NW, Room 300, Washington, DC 20036. 202-828-5170.

• "Dirty Business: Food Exports to the United States," 1990. About the flight of food processing companies to Mexico (with focus on Pillsbury-Green Giant), working conditions, and effects on the environment. $30. 15 minutes. Migrant Media Productions, P.O. Box 2048, Freedom, CA 95019. 408-728-8948.

• Interview with Santos Martinez, a leader of the Mexican Ford Workers Democratic Movement. English translation is dubbed over Martinez' voice. Also includes an interview with a Canadian Auto Workers local president. $25 US. 29 minutes. Windsor Occupational Safety and Health Group, 1731 Wyandotte St. E., Windsor, Ontario N8Y 1C9. 519-254-5157.

• "We Can Say No!" Describes how the U.S.-Canada Free Trade Agreement has hurt Canada and how to abrogate the Agreement. 28 minutes. "Fighting Back." Analysis of the U.S.-Canada FTA after its first two years. 60 minutes. Both videos are on one cassette. $34. Action Canada Network, Suite 904, 251 Laurier West, Ottawa, Ontario, K1P 5J6. 613-233-1764.

READINGS

• "Airlines: A Two-Tier Industry in Trouble," by Kim Moody. $2. Labor Notes, 7435 Michigan Ave., Detroit, MI 48210. 313-842-6262.

• *Briarpatch*, a Saskatchewan newsmagazine. Special 48-page issue on U.S.-Mexico-Canada free trade and efforts to build trinational solidarity. $4. Briarpatch, 2138 McIntyre St., Regina, Sask. S4P 2R7.

• *Catalogue of Publications 1991*. Lists publications on free trade, the economy, privatization, deregulation, employment, women and work. Canadian Centre for Policy Alternatives, #904-251 Laurier Avenue West, Ottawa, Ontario K1P 5J6. 613-563-1341.

• *Choosing Sides: Unions and the Team Concept*, by Mike Parker and Jane Slaughter. Explains management-by-stress. $15 plus $2 postage from Labor Notes, 7435 Michigan Ave., Detroit, MI 48210. 313-842-6262.

•

- *Coalition for Justice in the Maquiladoras* newsletter. Updates on the work of the Coalition, stockholders meetings, targeting multinational companies. $25/yr or member $15/yr. Border Project, Benedictine Resource Center, 530 Bandera Road, San Antonio, TX 78228. 512-735-4988.
- *Correspondencia*. A bilingual publication providing news and analysis on women's movements in Mexico, Canada, and the U.S. $10. Mujer a Mujer, P.O. Box 12322, San Antonio, TX 78212. 512-735-2629.
- "Crisis at our Doorstep: Occupational and Environmental Health Implications for Mexico-U.S.-Canada Trade Negotiations," 1991. 34 pages. $15 plus $3 postage. National Safe Workplace Institute, 122 S. Michigan Ave., Suite 1450, Chicago, IL 60603. 312-939-0690.
- *Cross Border Links*. Directory of educational, academic, social activist, labor, and business organizations with a special interest in cross-border relations in North America. Resource Center, Box 4506, Albuquerque, NM 87196. 505-842-8288.
- *Distorted Development: Mexico in the World Economy*, by David Barkin. An in-depth analysis of changes in the Mexican economy with free trade. David Barkin, Series in Political Economy and Economic Development in Latin America, Westview Press, Colorado, 1990. Call your local bookstore to order.
- "Exploiting Both Sides" and "Maquiladoras and Toxics," reports on workers' rights and environmental issues, and copies of Congressional testimony against free trade. Available from the AFL-CIO, 815 16th St. NW, Washington, DC 20006. 202-637-5000.
- "From the Yukon to the Yucatan: Free trade goes continental, so must labor solidarity," by Mary McGinn and Kim Moody, in the November 1991 issue of *Dollars & Sense*. Copies available from Labor Notes.
- "Global Village vs. Global Pillage: A One-World Strategy for Labor," by Jeremy Brecher and Tim Costello. Examines the globalization of the economy and union strategies. $3.75. International Labor Rights Education and Research Fund, 100 Maryland Ave. NE, Washington, DC 20002.
- *Labor in a Global Economy: Perspectives from the U.S. and Canada*. Collection of papers presented at conference held by the University of Oregon Labor Center, Eugene, OR 97403. Contributors include Larry Cohen, CWA; Jose LaLuz, ACTWU; Karen Nussbaum, 9-to-5; Katie Quan, ILGWU; Shirley Carr, Canadian Labour Congress; Elaine Bernard, Harvard Trade Union Program; and others. $15/$1.50 postage.
- *Latin American Labor News*. Published twice yearly. $15 for individuals. Center for Labor Research and Studies, Florida International University, University Park-W MO TR #2, Miami, FL 33199.
- "Mexico-U.S. Free Trade Negotiations and the Environment: Exploring the Issues." $10. Texas Center for Policy Studies, P.O. Box 2618, Austin, TX 78701.
- *The Other Side of Mexico*. English language newsletter on politics, human rights, and social movements. $15/yr for individuals, $20/yr for institutions, for 6 issues. Checks payable to "Carlos A. Heredia/Equipo Pueblo." A.P. 27-467, Mexico, D.F., Mexico 06760.
- Reprints of many articles on free trade and environmental concerns are available from the Institute for Agriculture and Trade Policy, 1313 Fifth St. SE, Suite 303, Minneapolis, MN 55414. Prices vary, $.50-$6.50.
- *Rethinking Columbus: Teaching about the 500th Anniversary of Columbus' Arrival in America*. This 100-page guide includes stories, poems, and essays which ex-

press a different view of the "discovery" of the "New World." $4 plus $2 postage. From the educational journal *Rethinking Schools*, 1001 E. Keefe Ave., Milwaukee, WI 53212. 414-964-9646.

• *SIPRO*, a Mexico City information center and clipping service, puts news and analysis on Mexican social and labor movements on PeaceNet's carnet.mexnews conference every week or so. PeaceNet subscribers should look for it.

• "Three Years of U.S.-Canada Free Trade," by Bruce Campbell, former economist for the Canadian Labour Confederation. Single issue: $3.50 or sub price: $24.50 regular, $35 organizations. *Canadian Dimension*, 707-228 Notre Dame Ave., Winnipeg, Manitoba, R3B 1N7. 204-957-1519.

• *A Troublemaker's Handbook: How To Fight Back Where You Work—and Win!* by Dan La Botz. An organizer's manual of winning strategies, from the shop floor to corporate campaigns. $17 plus $2 postage from Labor Notes.

• Two journals in Mexico have produced special issues in Spanish on the NAFTA. Both include views of Mexican, U.S., and Canadian labor leaders. One article in edition 5-6 of the journal *Trabajo* is an interview with representatives of five Mexican labor organizations (CTM, FAT, SNTE, CNTE, and SME). The five were among those who attended a trinational exchange with U.S. and Canadian labor leaders in April 1991 in Chicago. Copies in Spanish available for $3.50 from ALEC (see VIDEOS above). *Trabajo*, A.P. 22549, Tlalpan, C.P. 14000, Mexico, D.F., Mexico. Fax: (011) 52-5-686-8966. *El Cotidiano* (edition 43), A.P. 32-031, C.P. 06031, Mexico, D.F., Mexico. Phone: (011) 52-5-382-5000, ext. 151.

• *Trading Freedom: How Free Trade Affects Our Lives, Work, and Environment.* Contributors from the U.S., Mexico, and Canada critique the NAFTA and propose alternatives. $10 plus $3.50 postage. Institute for Policy Studies and Food First Books, 145 Ninth St., San Francisco, CA 94103. 800-888-3314.

• "Unceasing Abuses: Human Rights in Mexico One Year After the Introduction of Reforms," by Americas Watch. 35 pages. $5. Human Rights Watch, 485 Fifth Ave., New York, NY 10017.

T-SHIRTS

• "$4 a Day? No Way!/¿$4 Dolares por Jornada? ¡Para Nada!" bilingual t-shirts. Lettering in gold, on red or black shirts, large, extra-large and XXL (sizes run small). $10 plus 15% for shipping. ALEC, 2000 P St. NW, Suite 300, Washington, DC 20036. 202-828-5173.

COMPUTER NETWORK

PeaceNet is a network that enables users to communicate and exchange information quickly by computer. A subscription costs only $10/month, plus $6 to $10/hour. Since it takes just minutes to send messages or download information, the cost is small. Institute for Global Communications, 3228 Sacramento St., San Francisco, CA 94115. 415-923-0900.

CONTACTS IN THE U.S.

American Friends Service Committee, 1501 Cherry St., Philadelphia, PA 19102. 215-241-7132. Works with women in maquiladoras on U.S.-Mexico border, produces educational material on working women, and documents human rights violations against Mexicans on both sides of border. Periodic mailings on free trade.

Central America Labor Defense Network (CALDN), Box 28014, Oakland, CA 94604. 415-272-9951. Sends telegrams and letters of protest from U.S. unionists in cases of labor repression, disappearances, prisoners, in Central America and Mexico

Coalition for Justice in the Maquiladoras, c/o Interfaith Center on Corporate Responsibility, Room 566, 475 Riverside Dr., New York, NY 10115. 212-870-2295. A coalition of over 82 unions and religious, environmental, peace and justice, and Latino organizations that encourage U.S. transnationals to adopt "Standards of Conduct."

Fair Trade Coalitions exist in San Francisco, Los Angeles, St. Paul, Oakland, Kansas City, Washington, DC, Seattle, San Antonio, and Chicago. They include local labor, environmental, citizens, women's and community organizations. Primary work is public education on free trade. Call Network for U.S.-Mexico-Canada Labor Solidarity for contacts (see below).

Farm Labor Organizing Committee, 507 S. Saint Clair St., Toledo, OH 43602. 419-243-3456.

Federation for Industrial Retention and Renewal (FIRR), MCLR, 3411 W. Diversey, #14, Chicago, IL 60647. 312-252-7676. Active in Fair Trade Coalition. Works with unionists and communities on plant closures.

International Labor Rights Education and Research Fund, 100 Maryland Ave., NE, Washington DC, 20002. 202-544-7198. Researches labor rights violations in Mexico and pressures Congress for labor and environmental rights in Free Trade Agreement.

Labor Notes, 7435 Michigan Ave., Detroit , MI 48210. 313-842-6262. Fax: 842-0227. Acts as a networking center for unionists on a host of issues, including international solidarity and team concept. Sponsors conferences and tours. Monthly newsletter contains international labor news.

Maquiladora Task Force, UAW City CAP Council, 3141 North Oak Trafficway, Kansas City, MO 64116. 816-921-6881. Coalition of unions and others promoting labor and environmental rights on U.S.-Mexico border.

Mexico-U.S. Dialogos, 51 8th Ave., Brooklyn, NY 11217. 718-230-3628. Organizes conferences of labor (auto, telecommunications, farm worker) and political leaders from the U.S., Mexico, and Canada.

MEXUSCAN Task Force, United Auto Workers Local 879, 2191 Ford Parkway, St. Paul, MN 55116. 612-699-4246.

Mobilization on Development, Trade, Labor and the Environment (MODTLE), 100 Maryland Ave. NE, Room 502, Washington, DC 20002. 202-544-7198. Represents over 15 organizations, including labor, environmental, lobby, trade and development experts, and citizens groups.

National Network for Immigrant and Refugee Rights, 310 8th St., Suite 307, Oakland, CA 94607. 415-465-1984.

Network for U.S.-Mexico-Canada Labor Solidarity, c/o American Labor Education Center, 2000 P St. NW, Suite 300, Washington, DC 20036. 202-828-5173. A broad network of U.S. unionists interested in developing direct contact and mutual support with workers in Mexico and Canada, and providing information to local unions and community-labor organizations. The network has produced bi-monthly mailings with news and analysis of free trade in all three countries.

Trabajadores Desplazados/Displaced Workers of Green Giant, 434 Main St., #222, Watsonville, CA 95076. For more information call Teamsters Local 912 at 408-724-0683.

Transnationals Information Exchange (TIE-US), 7435 Michigan Ave., Detroit, MI 48210. 313-842-6262. Conferences, information exchange, and strategic planning among unionists in Mexico, Canada, and U.S. Focus on auto and telecommunications workers.

CONTACTS IN CANADA

Action Canada Network, Suite 904, 251 Laurier West, Ottawa, Ontario K1P 5J6. 613-233-1764. Network of over 50 national organizations and regional coalitions organizing to abrogate the U.S.-Canada Free Trade Agreement. Source for contacts, speakers, educational information.

Canadian Auto Workers, 205 Placer Court, North York, Willowdale, Ontario M2H 3H9. 416-497-4110. Provides free trade news from Canada and its impact for auto workers. Establishing direct links with U.S. and Mexican auto workers.

Common Frontiers, 11 Madison Ave., Toronto, Ontario M5R 2S2. 416-961-7847. Promotes education, research, and alliances with counterpart labor, environmental, women's, and religious groups in U.S. and Mexico.

Latin American Working Group, Box 2207, Station P, Toronto, Ontario M5S 2T2. 416-533-9940. Research and education on Latin American issues and their relevance to Canada. Produced LAWG Letter on Free Trade.

National Action Committee on the Status of Women (NAC), 344 Bloor St. West, Suite 505, Toronto, Ontario M5S 1W9. Coalition of over 500 Canadian women's organizations.

CONTACTS IN MEXICO

Centro de Información Laboral y Asesoría Sindical/Center for Labor Research and Union Support (CILAS), Dr. Liceaga 180 A-5 Despacho 1001, Colonia Doctores, Mexico, D.F., Mexico. (011)52-5-761-1126. Research and legal advice to independent unions and democratic trends within government-controlled Mexican unions. Active in building trinational links with auto and telecommunications workers.

Frente Autentico del Trabajo/Authentic Workers' Front (FAT), Godard No. 20, Colonia Guadalupe Victoria, 07790 Mexico, D.F., Mexico. (011)52-5-556-9375. 30-year old independent union federation representing small and medium-size Mexican businesses. Key in trinational links.

Mexican Action Network on Free Trade (RMALC in Spanish), c/o FAT, Godard No. 20, Colonia Guadalupe Victoria, 07790 Mexico, D.F., Mexico. (011)52-5-556-9375. National network of labor, environmental, women's, and political organizations against free trade.

Mujer a Mujer/Woman to Woman, A.P. 24-553, Colonia Roma, 06700 Mexico, D.F. (011)52-5-207-0834. Promotes communication and exchange among women in Mexico, U.S., and Canada.

Mujeres en Acción Sindical/Women in Union Action, Xola 1454, Colonia Narvarte, 03020 Mexico, D.F., Mexico. (011)52-5-519-8048. Provides leadership workshops for union women on labor law, health and safety, domestic work, and women's perspective on free trade.

Bibliography

BOOKS

- David Barkin, *Distorted Development: Mexico in the World Economy*, Westview Press, 1990.
- Burton Bendiner, *International Labour Affairs: The World Trade Unions and the Multinational Companies*, Clarendon Press, 1987.
- Jeremy Brecher and Tim Costello, *Global Village vs. Global Pillage: A One-World Strategy for Labor*, International Labor Rights Education and Research Fund, 1991.
- Nicholas Colchester and David Buchan, *Europower: The Essential Guide to Europe's Economic Transformation in 1992*, Random House, 1990.
- Charles Craypo, *The Economics of Collective Bargaining*, Bureau of National Affairs, 1986.
- Paul Stephen Dempsey, *Flying Blind: The Failure of Airline Deregulation*, Economic Policy Institute, 1990.
- *Economic Report of the President*, 1986, 1988, 1991.
- Jeff Faux and Richard Rothstein, *Fast Track, Fast Shuffle*, Economic Policy Institute, 1991.
- William Glade and Cassio Luiselli, *The Economics of Interdependence: Mexico and the United States*, University of California, San Diego, 1989.
- John Grahl and Paul Teague, *1992—The Big Market: The Future of the European Community*, Lawrence & Wishart, 1990.
- Nigel Grimwade, *International Trade: New Patterns of Trade, Production and Investment*, Routledge, 1990.
- Joseph Grunwald and Kenneth Flamm, *The Global Factory: Foreign Assembly in International Trade*, Brookings Institution, 1985.
- Bennett Harrison and Barry Bluestone, *The Great U-Turn: Corporate Restructuring and the Polarization of America*, Basic Books, 1988.
- Steven Hecker and Margaret Hallock, *Labor in a Global Economy*, University of Oregon Books, 1991.
- DeAnne Julius, *Global Companies and Public Policy: The Growing Challenge of Foreign Direct Investment*, Pinter Publishers, 1990.
- Dan La Botz, *The Crisis of Mexican Labor*, Praeger, 1988.
- Dan La Botz, *Rank and File Rebellion: Teamsters for a Democratic Union*, Verso, 1990.
- Dan La Botz, *A Troublemaker's Handbook: How To Fight Back Where You Work—And Win*, Labor Notes, 1991.
- Arthur MacEwan, *Debt and Disorder: International Economic Instability and U.S. Imperial Decline*, Monthly Review Press, 1990.
- Kim Moody, *An Injury To All: The Decline of American Unionism*, Verso, 1988.
- Mike Parker and Jane Slaughter, *Choosing Sides: Unions and the Team Concept*, Labor Notes, 1988.
- Mike Parker and Jane Slaughter, *The Search for Job Security: UAW Bargaining in 1990*, Labor Notes, 1990.
- Harley Shaiken, *Mexico In The Global Economy*, University of California, San Diego, 1990.
- U.S. Bureau of Labor Statistics, *Handbook of Labor Statistics*, 1989.

82

- U.S. Department of Commerce, *U.S. Industrial Outlook*, 1991.
- U.S. Department of Commerce, *Statistical Abstract of the United States*, 1991.
- Peter Waterman, *For A New Labour Internationalism*, International Labour Education, Research, and Information Foundation, Netherlands, 1984.
- James P. Womack, Daniel T. Jones, and Daniel Roos, *The Machine That Changed the World*, Rawson Associates, 1990.
- *The World Almanac*, Pharos Books, 1991.
- *World Development Report*, World Bank, 1991.

REPORTS AND STUDIES

- Action Canada Network, "The First Two Years of Free Trade," Ottawa, 1991.
- AFL-CIO, "Exploiting Both Sides: U.S.-Mexico Free Trade," 1991.
- William Ambrose, Paul Hennermeyer, and Jean-Paul Chapon, "Privatizing Telecommunications Systems," International Finance Corporation/World Bank, Discussion Paper 10, 1990.
- American Labor Education Center, "$4 A Day, No Way," 1991.
- American Labor Education Center, "Some Facts About Mexico," 1990.
- Thomas Bailey and Theo Eicher, "The Effect of the North American Free Trade Agreement on Apparel Employment in the U.S.," Bureau of International Labor Affairs, U.S. Department of Labor, 1991.
- B.C. Working Group on Canada-Mexico Free Trade, "Que Pasa? A Canada-Mexico 'Free' Trade Deal: Impact on British Columbia," 1990.
- "California's Stake in the U.S.-Mexico Trade Negotiations," California State World Trade Commission, January 31, 1991.
- Duncan Cameron, "Questions and Answers on the Free Trade Agreement," Canadian Centre for Policy Alternatives, Ottawa, 1989.
- Centro de Investigación Laboral y Asesoría Sindical, A.C., "Big Three Employment in Mexico," Mexico City, 1991.
- CWA Information Industry Reports, March 1991, August 1991.
- CWA Report on Recent Developments in the U.S. Telecom Industry, August 1991.
- Judy Fudge, "Background Notes on Mexico," National Action Committee on the Status of Women, Toronto, June 14, 1991.
- Stephen Herzenberg, "The Internationalization of the Auto Parts Industry, 1958-87 and Beyond," draft, U.S. Department of Labor, 1989.
- Stephen Herzenberg, "The North American Auto Industry at the Onset of Continental Free Trade Negotiations," draft, U.S. Department of Labor, 1991.
- Stephen Herzenberg and Harley Shaiken, "Labor Market Segmentation in the North American Auto Industry," mimeo, 1990.
- Andrew Jackson, "Job Losses in Canadian Manufacturing, 1989-1991," Canadian Centre for Policy Alternatives, 1991.
- Yannis Karmokolias, "Automotive Industry Trends and Prospects for Investment in Developing Countries," Discussion Paper 7, International Finance Corporation and World Bank, 1990.
- Timothy Koechlin, Mehrene Larudee, Samuel Bowles, and Gerald Epstein, "Estimates of the Impact of the Free Trade Agreement on Direct U.S. Investment in Mexico," mimeo, Testimony to the U.S. Trade Representative, September 11, 1991.
- Labor Institute, "Preliminary Analysis of Wisconsin Local Leaders Surveys," 1990.

- "The Likely Impact on the United States of a Free Trade Agreement with Mexico," U.S. International Trade Commission, Publication 2353, 1991.
- Jordy Micheli, "The Recent Development of the Car Industry in Mexico: Two Strategic Issues," mimeo, 1990.
- Kim Moody, "Airlines: A Two-Tier Industry in Trouble," Labor Notes, 1990.
- Mujer a Mujer, "A Brief Outline On Women's Situation and Struggles in Mexico," Mexico City, 1991.
- National Action Committee on the Status of Women, "Free Trade: A Bad Deal for Women," 1988.
- National Action Committee on the Status of Women, "What Every Woman Needs to Know About Free Trade," Toronto, 1988.
- New Democratic Party's Minority Report on North American Free Trade, December 20, 1990.
- Richard Nolan, Submission to the House of Commons Special Committee on Canada-United States Air Transportation Services, Canadian Union of Public Employees, December 11, 1990.
- Office of the U.S. Trade Representative, "1991 Trade Policy Review and 1990 Annual Report of the President of the United States on the Trade Agreements Program," 1991.
- Rick Salutin, "What Kind of Canada: Our Culture Is Not Protected Under this Deal as Promised," The Facts, Canadian Union of Public Employees, Spring 1988.
- Standard & Poor, "Aerospace & Air Transport," Industry Surveys, June 20, 1991.
- Telecommunications Workers Union, "The Future of Canada's Telecommunications System: Canadians Have A Choice," 1990.
- U.S. Bureau of Labor Statistics, International Wage Comparisons, 1991.
- U.S. Department of Commerce, U.S. Telecommunications in a Global Economy: Competitiveness at a Crossroads, 1990.
- Ben Watanabe, "Japanese Workers—Karoshi," unpublished, 1991.
- World Bank, Mexico: Towards Growth, Structural Reform and Macroeconomic Stability in Mexico, Volumes 1 and 2, 1988.

PERIODICALS

Air Transport World
The Autoworker, UAW Local 879
Aviation Daily
Aviation Week and Space Technology
Boston Globe
Briarpatch
The Brookings Review
Business Week
Canadian Dimension
CLC Today,
    Canadian Labour Congress
Dollars and Sense
Earth Island Journal
Economic Justice Report, Ecumenical
    Coalition for Economic Justice,
    Toronto

The Economist
El Financiero, Mexico City
Financial Post, Toronto
Flightlog, Association of Flight
    Attendants
Globe and Mail, Toronto
Guardian
Label Letter, AFL-CIO Union Label
    and Services Department
Labor Notes
Labor Studies Forum, University and
    College Labor Education Association
LAWG LETTER, Latin American
    Working Group, Toronto
Los Angeles Times
Monthly Labor Review

Multinational Monitor
NACLA Report, North American
  Committee on Latin America
New York Times
The Other Side of Mexico
Our Times, Toronto
The Plane Truth
Solidarity, United Auto Workers
State Worker, Communications
  Workers of America
This Magazine, Toronto

Trabajo, Mexico City
Traffic World
Unity, Airline Division, Canadian
  Union of Public Employees
Uno Más Uno, Mexico City
U.S.-Mexico Free Trade Reporter,
  Washington, D.C.
The Washington Post Weekly Edition
UAW Washington Report
Wall Street Journal

DOCUMENTS, RELEASES AND LEAFLETS

- Action Canada Network-Alberta, "Brian Mulroney Must Resign," Edmonton, June 1, 1991.
- Canadian Auto Workers, "Free Trade Facts," Vol. 21, No. 13, April 12, 1991.
- Canadian Auto Workers, "International Union Coalition Sends Message to Northern Telecom," October 25, 1991.
- Canadian Union of Public Employees, "The Facts on Free Trade: Canada, Don't Trade It Away," Ottawa, 1988.
- Comisión de Modernización, STRM, "Circular Informativa," 21 julio, 1990.
- Farm Labor Organizing Committee, "U.S.-Mexico Exchange," 1990.
- Tony Mazzocchi, "Become a Labor Party Advocate," Labor Party Advocates, 1991.
- Pro-Canada Network, "What's the Big Deal? Some Straightforward Questions and Answers on Free Trade," Ottawa, 1988.
- "Stitching Solidarity Together," Pro-Canada Dossier #29, 1991.
- Trabajadores Desplazados, "Boycott Pillsbury-Green Giant," 1991.
- U.S. Department of Transportation, "Remarks Prepared for Delivery by Secretary of Transportation Samuel Skinner," June 20, 1991.